"Until Next Time...
Good Selling!"

Pat!

Proud to have
you as my friend

Ray Ohlson

Raymond J. Ohlson, CLU

First published by Dog Ear Publishing
4010 W. 86th Street, Ste H
Indianapolis, IN 46268
www.dogearpublishing.net

ISBN: 1-59858-116-3
Library of Congress Control Number: 2006920011

This book is printed on acid-free paper.

Printed in the United States of America

Preface

"Bent, but not broken" is my way of describing the photograph on the cover of this book. This palm tree is located in the backyard of my beach villa in South Carolina. We have owned this home since the early 1980s. You can see that this palm tree has weathered driving rains, tropical storm winds, and hurricanes, but it never gave up. It never fell, and it will be there well into the next decades. It's my favorite foliage. It reminds me that a firm foundation—a strong base—and a commitment to not giving in is what it's all about in our business *and* in our lives. Many of my writings were inspired by that fact and by that bent but unbroken palm tree.

I was fortunate to start selling life insurance while I was completing my bachelor's degree at Ball State University. My degree is in Radio, Television, and Motion Pictures with a minor in Journalism. Those were the fields I thought I would pursue. But, qualifying as a provisional applicant to the Million Dollar Round Table (MDRT) immediately following graduation convinced me to "give the business a try." What a lucky break! I've had the great fortune to be a Life Member of Million Dollar Round Table (MDRT), to receive my Chartered Life Underwriter (CLU) designation from the American College, to become an agency builder, to be elected president of two US life insurance companies, and to serve as chief marketing officer for a Luxembourg and Bermuda carrier.

Following these challenging experiences, I re-opened The Ohlson Group, Inc., and we now again market insurance and financial services products through professional insurance agents and advisors all across America! Income is higher than it's ever been, I have a great staff, I'm having fun, and I get to spend more time with my beautiful wife Ann and our three adult children, Nick, Joe, and Kiley.

I am lucky to be in the greatest business in the world and blessed to have been on both sides of the fence. The following pages represent many of my weekly writings over the past few years. They are thoughts on life and our business. They are meant to stop us in our tracks and cause us to reflect on what's really important in life. Also, I hope they provide ideas on how to enjoy our lives better while increasing our income and solidifying our careers.

I hope you enjoy this book and that it will assist you in planning for the future. I am certain that many of you have encountered the same type of pressure that my favorite palm tree has survived. Let this book assist you in having the same strength and fortitude that the palm tree owns. We may bend, but never break!

Thanks for taking the time to read and listen. Until next time...
GOOD SELLING!

Raymond J. Ohlson, CLU
Carmel, Indiana

Acknowledgements

I've had many friends, family members, and mentors who have contributed to my success. There are too many to mention in this book, but I would be remiss if I didn't mention some very important people.

Benjamin "Woody" Woodson, former Chairman, American General Life, a true role model; George Beatrice, friend, supervisor, and mentor; Bob Rever, former President, American General who believed in me early in my career. Friends like Tom and Jan Lazzara, my great office staff, my parents, Cal and Mary, who instilled a work ethic in me, my brother Jim, sister Kathy, and so many others who gave me the stamina and desire to succeed. But most of all, my thanks to the most beautiful, brilliant, and supportive person in the world—my wife, Ann. She is always there and is the love of my life. Also, thanks to my kids—Nick, Joe, and Kiley—thanks for letting me be the dad I wanted to be. Thanks for keeping me in your lives and for treasuring "La Famiglia!"

Part I
Self-Improvement

Chapter 1

SCIP (*Service, Credibility, Integrity and Profitability*)

Several years ago I had the privilege of serving as president of a US life insurance company. It was an exciting though somewhat daunting endeavor. As most of you, I had spent all of my previous time in the field as a producer, agency manager, and owner of my own Midwestern insurance marketing organization. I swore that I would never work in an insurance company home office. I'm glad I had that opportunity to change my mind. It was a great time in my life.

I did have one problem, however. I had never been president of a life company. Consequently, I read, asked questions, and gathered as much insight as I could about this new and important position. I called on many people that I admired and trusted. They gave me much helpful information, but I was still looking for the concise advice that would allow me to feel comfortable about the awesome new tasks awaiting me.

Well, I found the answer. A great insurance company president gave me this advice.

"Ray," he said. "Running a life insurance company is like sitting on a three legged milk stool. All legs are important if you are going to develop the company in a fair and equitable manner. The three legs are, simply: the company, the agents, and the policyholders. We must treat them all with equal dignity and respect. If you

start shaving corners off the legs, you will find yourself with your butt on the ground! Tell the truth and tell the same story to all."

This was simple yet wonderful advice. I did my best to keep this analogy at the front of my mind as I grew into my new position. But, this was only part of the evaluation. What would be the principles I would use to make sure that I was operating in a prudent manner? I chose the following—please allow me to share.

SCIP

SCIP stands for: service, credibility, integrity, and profitability. These four attributes must be there for all—the company, the agents, <u>and</u> the policyholders. Short change any of the parties and you will no longer be on solid footing—your three-legged stool will tip over. Let's look at Webster's definition.

- **SERVICE**—a helpful or useful action; a benefit or advantage.
- **CREDIBILITY**—that can be believed, reliable.
- **INTEGRITY**—honesty, sincerity; completeness, and wholeness.
- **PROFITABILITY**—advantage, gain, financial gain; esp. the sum remaining after deducting costs.

Pretty simple, right? Well, unfortunately far too many business people aren't adhering to these principles nor following the implied mandates of these four attributes these days. The financial services industry is no exception.

There are always a few bad actors that detract from the exceptional benefits that we provide our clients, I suggest a periodic "self question- naire" to assist us in making important business decisions in <u>our</u> busi- ness. This self test will help each of us determine with whom we work (company and wholesaler), how we deal with our clients and carriers, and how all three parties (all three legs of the stool) can succeed in a profitable state.

Here are some examples of this self test—ask yourself these ques- tions:

- Do your present carriers treat old and new clients with equal respect?

- Are your present carriers financially solvent? Are they making a profit?
- Does your wholesaler offer more to you than products and compensation.
- Does he or she provide new marketing ideas?
- Does your wholesaler act as an "observation deck" for you? Keep you up to date on industry and tax law changes?
- Do you, as the agent, back up all promises made at the time of sale? They view that as part of the deal.
- Are you making a sufficient profit in the markets you work and in the way you conduct your business?

This isn't a lecture. I have to do this myself on a constant basis. Remember we are all tied together. We are customers and vendors to each other. Take some time to analyze your "three legged milk stool." Because, you are **_president_** of your <u>own</u> organization. **You control you!**

Service, Credibility, Integrity, & Profitability (SCIP)—it has to be there for all three parties. If SCIP is not there, the stool will eventually collapse.

Those were ten great years I spent as president of that company, but things haven't changed. I still offer a service. I hope it's viewed as a <u>quality</u> service. I hope I am perceived as providing it with credibility and integrity. And, like you, I need profitability—and so does <u>your</u> company and clients.

Life really is simpler and better when we all win!

Chapter 2

From Muncie To Milan

I graduated from Ball State University in Muncie, Indiana. I started my insurance career while a senior in college. The life insurance career was not something I dreamed about. It wasn't a thunderbolt at age 12 that led me to believe that I wanted to be a straight commissioned life insurance salesman. I was putting my way through college working in the car wash and playing bass guitar in a band. I met Ann, my wife, and decided I should try something with substance. My degree was in Radio, Television & Motion Pictures with a Journalism minor. Many would feel a far cry from what I do today.

Not really! I feel as though that training enabled me to embrace technology and the media. I've done radio and television shows promoting my work. I use email marketing and write, as you know, a weekly commentary. In other words, I adapt to the situation at hand. Find the common denominators and put them to work.

I've been fortunate to have held many positions in this great business of ours. Career Agent, Agency Manager, General Agent, Chief Marketing Officer, President of two life insurance companies and Chief Marketing Officer of a Luxembourg and Bermuda insurance company. I've been involved in raising over $100 million and helped take a company public. I was involved in a joint venture with an insurance company from Ukraine. I became friends with their CEO while communicating through an interpreter. Our U.S. company was $79 million in assets when purchased, was in a run-off position with no agents or products.

I led the charge building that company from $79 million to $1.7 billion. The same was true on the international side. The company was purchased for $2 million at a size of $70 million and sold at $750 million—8 years later for a 10 fold profit. Something special? I didn't think so. I just used the marketing skills that were taught to me over the years. I based everything on SCIP—Service, Credibility, Integrity and Profitability. Treat everyone with the same dignity and respect that you would want if the tables were reversed. Follow the Golden Rule. Simple? I think so.

Bottom line, I used the same marketing principle in Milan, Stockholm, Brussels, London and Holland that I used in Muncie, Indiana. So, how do I position myself? I position myself as a financial services professional with marketing skills that can be transmitted to my associates in the field. I have an ability to assist those to reach their personal levels of success regardless of where they live.

No bragging, no sound bytes, no *unbelievable claims*, just a past record that will stand the test of time and a plan that is designed to assist whether you are in New York, Paducah, San Francisco, Chicago or Peoria. I'm confident that I can assist you in your quest for success. Magic? Miracles? Something special? Not really, just good training, attention to detail and someone wanting to give back as much as I was given. Maybe that's the key. I believe I have an obligation to assist all desirous of reaching my perceived level of success. Isn't that what life is all about? Giving back? I think so. Try it…you'll like it!

Chapter 3

Where Does It Hurt?

When I was a child, if I didn't feel well, the doctor would ask me, "Where does it hurt?" Not much has changed in medicine. You make an appointment with your physician and he asks, "What's wrong? Where do you feel badly? Tell me about the pain. Is it constant? Do you have limitations? Is it keeping you up at nights? How long has this been going on?"

I'm sure these questions and statements are familiar to you. At least, I hope they are; otherwise, you should probably change physicians. You don't want your doctor to treat an ailment, prescribe medication, or order surgery before he knows what's going on. Do you? No! The doctor needs to know the answer to "where does it hurt." The same should be true in the financial services business. Let's examine to make sure we are following our own "Hippocratic Oath."

When you meet with your prospects and clients, are you getting a complete picture of their financial health? Are you asking where they "hurt financially?" Believe me, your clients do have some "ouchies." But, they are very proud when it comes to their financial health. They won't volunteer where it hurts unless you ask them. Ask them once, twice, or more. Because of their pride, financial illness can make them feel as though they brought on this ailment themselves. They may feel stupid when admitting to their economic pain. So, we have to pry. It's is not unlike what the doctor does when he brings in his chart. We bring in our fact finder. Or, at least we should.

There are many different kinds of financial pain. Some can be very evident. For example,

- Expenses too high—income too low;
- Excessive credit card debt;
- Significant losses in the equity market;
- High cost of prescription drugs and medical care;
- A new or unexpected, major expense—e.g., new roof, furnace, etc.

These "pains" are easy to diagnose, and the prescription for financial health somewhat easier. Control expenses, increase income, get a budget, and make a plan—lots of tough medicine here. But what about those harder to diagnose illnesses that keep them up at night?

One thing that comes with age is increased worry. It seems as though it should lessen, but it doesn't. Most people continue to worry about their kids, even after they are out of school and married. Granted, they are different worries, but they will keep us up at night! I speak from personal experience here! If we are lucky enough to have grandchildren, we can worry about them too. We hope they are healthy, do well in school, go to college, get a great job, marry a wonderful person, have kids, buy a wonderful home, and retire wealthy.

What about the great change in life expectancy? Today it is common to live well into our 80s and 90s. It's not unusual to hear about people living past 100! You talk about worry! These older Americans are asking, "Can I really afford to live that long? If I could only be assured that I will have the money. If I could only pass on a legacy to my kids and grandkids. If I didn't have to worry about the stock market when I watch the evening news. If only I could relax knowing that I am safe financially so I could finally get a good night's sleep!" These are the "pains" of aging that most elders aren't comfortable discussing with strangers.

We are part of your client's financial medical team! Let's make sure that we don't barge in, prescribe the fix while we have our hand on the office door, and leave. Our clients want to deal with:

- Someone they like—that's right—like!
- Someone they trust!
- Someone who will prescribe "SAFE" medicine and explain all of the potential side affects!
- Someone who will refer them to other professionals!
- Someone who will check back with them (a financial review)!

Our business can be much easier and much better if we treat people the way they expect their doctors to treat them. If we don't treat them in this manner, we shouldn't be surprised when they look for a second opinion.

So, ask the tough questions (in a friendly manner) and then sit back and shut up! You've heard it before: we have two ears and one mouth—so we should do TWICE as much listening. But, never forget: after the pleasantries, ask your client "Where does it hurt?" This is the proper way to begin the financial healing process!

Chapter 4

May I Help?

Isn't that what we are all trying to do? Help people? As financial services professionals, I know that's what we try to do every day. You want to help your clients achieve their goals by educating them and guiding them. You want the best for them because you know if you are successful, it's the old win-win situation.

Our business is exactly the same, except that <u>you</u> are our clients. And we want to:

- Help you help your client.
- Help you achieve the success levels that you are desirous of reaching.
- Help you make doing business with us easy.
- Help you by supplying information that will assist you in helping your client.

Did you notice that I haven't mentioned products or commissions? I haven't talked about trips, bonuses, services, or incentives. WHY? Everybody can offer these things. Let's face it. Most products and compensation packages are about the same. All customers should and do expect world-class service. It's the other things that help you in your personal and professional life that make a difference.

So, what about you? What are you offering your clients? A better annuity? I'm sure that your competition will try to convince your client that theirs is better. Higher interest rates? Better participation rates? Remember the old adage: live by the sword; die by the sword!

Rather than worrying about the obvious, remember these things first: you are *helping* your client navigate through their retirement years. You are *helping* them hold on to their principal. You are *helping* them pass it down to their named beneficiaries. You are *helping* them keep Uncle Sam's paws off the dough. You are *helping* them bypass probate. You are *helping* them by providing an income stream that they cannot outlive.

Doesn't that sound like you are offering a lot more than the typical "product" sales person? You are not asking for a sale; you are asking, "May I help you?" Good things DO happen to good people. People like to do business with good people. People who help are good people. I hope that in some small way, I have helped you.

Chapter 5

Credibility and Integrity

As I wrote in Chapter 1, SCIP™ stands for SERVICE, CREDIBILITY, INTEGRITY and PROFITABILITY. These are the cornerstones upon which I've attempted to live my personal and professional life. I used these principles as a career agent, a general agent, a president of a life insurance company, and an owner of an Insurance Marketing Organization (IMO). I believe that adherence to these four words makes our life easier, more enjoyable, and much more profitable. I continue to research these words, examine the definitions, apply them to my business, and do a "self test" to see if I am truly "putting my money where my mouth is." But, I find in my talks and writings, that my audience often becomes confused with the definitions. I find that many of us put "credibility" and "integrity" in the same camp. Nothing could be further from the truth. Allow me to explain.

CREDIBILITY, in its simplest definition, is "believability" or the ability to "instill" belief in a person, organization, or concept. It also leads one to believe that a credible person is "dependable." We have many examples of this in our personal lives. An example could be your dry cleaner—"24 hour service—shirts in by 8AM this morning, back by the next day." It's also as simple as people being on time, items delivered as promised. UPS and FedEx are perfect examples of CREDIBILITY. They deliver as promised. There are many people in our lives who we perceive as credible. Examples are politicians, business leaders, sales professionals, physicians, men and women of the cloth, and others. But we have many examples when we have felt betrayed and surprised to discover that one of our "credible" people has been less than honest. We see business leaders standing trial, some going to jail; dishonest politicians and possibly friends who are exposed in less than honest situations. Does that mean that they were not and are not credible? Surprisingly, the answer is "no." To the contrary, they were credible, but their lack of honesty destroyed their believability in an instant. Let's look at the difference between CREDIBILITY and INTEGRITY.

INTEGRITY is honesty. That's the difference. A person or organization with integrity always conducts itself in an honest way. They are your perfect partners in your business and personal life. We have all heard about the "snake oil salesmen." They come into town with CREDIBILITY. They were believable. They instilled belief. But they sold ointments and elixirs that were bogus. But people bought from them. WHY? They were credible. When the snake oil salesman left town, the people found that the magic potion was worthless. His CREDIBILITY vanished. WHY? He had no INTEGRITY—no honesty.

A person with INTEGRITY is not always credible. I know many honest people on whom I can't always depend. They are not bad. They just forget things; they aren't on time; or they don't follow through. But, they are people of INTEGRITY. Have I confused you yet? You are probably wondering where I am going with this.

Okay, the perfect recipe is to do business with people and organizations that are full of CREDIBILITY and INTEGRITY. You can depend on these people, and you will always know that what they do or say will be honest. The big difference between CREDIBILITY and INTEGRIY is as follows: I believe that you are born with INTEGRITY and you fight to keep on the right or honest side of all endeavors. CREDIBILITY, on the other hand, is something that you must earn. In some cases, it takes years to finally acquire and to be known as the "go to person"—the dependable one. But, regardless of how long it took to attain that stature, it can all disappear in an instant. It takes a great deal of work and attention to detail to remain CREDIBLE. It takes following "the Golden Rule" to maintain INTEGRITY. So, my final bit of preaching is:

- Don't make promises that you can't keep.
- Treat people with the same dignity and respect that you would want if the tables were reversed. And finally,
- Strive to always do what's right.

Not a fancy business plan, but these are the reasons people do business with us and why people want to be our friends. SERVICE, CREDIBILITY, INTEGRITY and PROFITABILITY (SCIP™)—it's got to be there for EVERYBODY!

Chapter 6

The Right Thing To Do

You've probably heard or read that, "Management is doing the right things." I really believe that statement is so true. I've followed that statement in my thirty years in the field managing an agency, running my marketing organization, as president of a US life insurance company, and in my role as chief marketing officer for an international financial services company. Life is a lot easier if you "talk the talk and walk the walk."

Doing the right things has never been more important in our business than it is today. Scandals are popping up weekly in newspapers and magazines and on radio and television. The mutual fund industry is the most recent to fall from grace in the minds of investors. Trillions of dollars have been entrusted to these companies that manage money for large as well as average investors. Many of our clients and agents in the Senior Market have entrusted their faith in their mutual funds as well as into individual stocks of the recently tarnished behemoth organizations. Why did all this happen? Was it greed? Many of the companies appeared to be making money. They didn't have to cross the line. Evidently, they were doing most things right but not doing the right things. Consequently, they've lost the faith of millions of American investors and savers. But therein is our opportunity!

We are in a position to give financial advice on a daily basis. Much of the decision making, provided by the client, rests in their trust in you. This trust is developed very quickly and carries with it an enormous responsibility to do the right things. What exactly does that mean? Give them the "Mom & Dad Test"—would you offer your product to your mother or father?

If your answer is, "no," put that brochure back into your briefcase and find another. The access to and availability of quality annuity and life products is tremendous.

I'm not suggesting that you start promoting "no load" products. You have to make a living and must be compensated for your services.

Your service is what separates you from the "Buy Direct" companies. But, there are quality products without loopholes, without traps, without two-tiered interest crediting concepts, and without restrictive payouts at death or surrender. These quality products will allow you to sleep well at night, avoid that bone-chilling complaint letter from the insurance department, or the threat of a lawsuit from a disgruntled beneficiary.

Life insurance companies will be reviewing their practices and product lines (believe me, I've been in those gut-wrenching meetings where insurance companies make quick, often knee-jerk decisions when they are nervous). They are, or will be, nervous soon enough. Suitability requirements, selling restrictions in certain states, and the fear of bad press will make them take action. Maybe some of those companies were doing things right (issuing policies, paying of commissions, etc), but were they doing the right things?

So, in our company, are redoubling our efforts to continue to do the right things. Oh, we will continue and strive to do things right when it comes to services and support, but we will promote quality products through financially strong, qualified carriers. I am confident that this strategy will provide all of us with a mutually profitable relationship.

Please don't take this commentary as a lecture. Take it as my opinion based upon many successful years in this business. Both inside the home office and outside with you. So, give your products the "Mom & Dad Test." If they don't stand up to the test, get rid of them and find new ones! Believe me, you will be doing the right thing.

Chapter 7

Success Phobia

Millions of people have phobias. There is fear of flying, fear of heights, fear of spiders, and many more. These are real fears. It's easy not to understand if you don't experience these fears. Let's look at the definition of "phobia" according to Webster: "*to be frightened: an exaggerated, usually inexplicable and illogical fear of a particular object or class of object.*"

Webster is correct. A phobia is an illogical fear, but nonetheless, it exists. A frequent flyer may have difficulty understanding another individual's fear of flying. The person with this fear understands, intellectually, that flying is safer than driving, but he or she is still scared. Physicians may prescribe medication or therapy to assist the person in coping with or conquering a phobia. I'm not sure of the rate of success, but I know that it helps many.

What about the fear of success? Have you ever heard of someone fearing success? Sounds illogical doesn't it? Nonetheless, it exists. It's there in every walk of life. It exists on both a professional and a personal level. Success carries with it great responsibilities. It requires constant attention and adjustments to the plan.

The quest for success can also be lonely. You are usually in the quest by yourself. Furthermore, you must deal with the quest for success on a 24/7 basis. Plus, you may experience an additional fear of *maintaining* the success. The first taste of success is the easiest. *Staying* successful is the challenge. We've all heard of the "one hit wonders." This question is at the heart of the fear of success: "can I maintain that status?" The real questions should revolve around alternatives to becoming successful. Allow me to explain.

Not striving for success is more difficult. It may be easier, physically, to avoid the quest, but it is not easier mentally. Lack of success can bring about low self esteem, lack of true happiness, and a lack of purpose. So what can a person do if he/or she suffers from what I call "success phobia?"

The first step is therapy, not with a medical professional, but rather with a trusted associate, a friend, or a mentor. Some people may not feel comfortable bearing their soul to an associate or friend. So let's find the mentor. Let's find someone who Napoleon Hill would describe as a member of your "Master Mind Group." These are people that are sympathetic and empathetic with your hopes, dreams, and desires. A person from this group should be someone who benefits from your success, a person who can benefit financially from your success in a business situation. Engaging in a solid, analytical discussion and developing a game plan may bring you the necessary confidence you need to conquer your fear of success.

Though some may believe that it is impossible to fear success because it just seems so illogical, they should remember the definition of a phobia. A phobia is illogical; therefore, if we call fearing success a kind of phobia, then it is illogical.

If you think you may be afraid of succeeding, consider the alternatives—find a mentor, someone to guide you and help you overcome your illogical phobia. The rewards will be worth the additional time, planning, and work that you put into this endeavor.

Chapter 8

The Changing Tides

My family and I enjoy spending some time together at our beach house in South Carolina. These are precious moments for us. Nick, our oldest, now works with me and Joe and Kiley are in college. Ann, my wife, and I are thankful for each summer vacation when we can all be together. Life gets a little more complicated each year. I fear that it will prove increasingly difficult to get everyone together in the very near future. The kids will have full time jobs and possibly families and other commitments that will prove difficult when trying to schedule a "family reunion." But, I am enjoying every day that we have together. It makes all the hard work well worthwhile!

This summer respite is always beneficial to me when analyzing the past and planning for the future. My mind runs free when I'm walking the beach and observing all of nature's beauty without deadlines to meet or a schedule to adhere to. I always return home with renewed conviction, increased energy, and a clear head when tackling the tasks at hand. I'm ready to embrace the changes that lie ahead and I know that there will be plenty.

It has often been said that one constant in our lives is that there will always be change. The changing tides and shifting sands on the beach are a verification of this view. You see, there are four tidal changes everyday—two high and two low. The height and the low point of the tides are determined by many different factors. They are basically, the moon, the wind, and disturbances at sea. A strong sea that produces a very high tide may bring sticks, limbs, and other ocean debris onto the beach. Strong storms may even cause serious erosion and take away some of the beach's beauty. Some are so damaging that sand needs to be imported from the ocean and blown in to preserve the integrity of the beach and to protect the shoreline. These are immediate emergencies that call for immediate action to give all home dwellers and visitors that instant gratification that they so dearly expect.

But, what would happen if we allow nature to take its course without human intervention? Everything would be just fine over time. The beach would return, in most cases, to its original stature. The two high and two low tides bring the reeds and shells in and also take them back to sea. The high tide brings in additional sand to replenish.

I find many similarities in business. One could often hear the gnashing of teeth and the prognostications of gloom and doom when referring to our economy, or in recent years, our business. I believe that soft high tides are renourishing and replenishing our business, and the best days lie ahead of us. But, we must be able to recognize the opportunities and react accordingly. I believe that it is important to discuss your goals and brainstorm with trusted associates. That's what we do at my office. We choose to associate with professionals in the financial services arena who desire a *"strategic alliance with a quality marketing organization."* Not with just a brokerage house. No, they want to align with an organization that is truly sympathetic and empathetic with their goals and desires.

I referred earlier to the four tidal changes. They are easy to predict on the beach. They change every six hours. Anyone with a watch can figure that. But, what about the changing tides in business and industry? It's important, if not vital, that you align yourself with a marketing organization that has the experience, knowledge, and vision to see the changing tides as they sweep over our business. Rather than be buried in the shifting sands, you'll be ready to move forward, replenished and eager to take on the new challenges!

Chapter 9

Commentary: A Different Experience

Some have asked why I decided to use "…a different experience" as my tag line or moniker for The Ohlson Group, Inc. Well, here's the answer. I was looking for something simple to differentiate us from the other marketing organizations. I didn't want to say "Experience the Difference" or some other phrase that would seem braggadocios. I didn't want to say we were the best. Why? Don't know that we are and how do you prove it? So, I settled on "…a different experience." This does not imply that we are the biggest, best, smartest, or most successful. It just states that The Ohlson Group, Inc….IS a different experience. Please allow me to back up this statement.

My staff and I have a very diverse background in this industry. We have both street and "palace" (home office) experience. I spent my first twenty years earning an honest living on a 1099. I was then able to help direct the efforts of a US life insurance company as its president and an international company as chief marketing officer. I ventured back to the field to re-open The Ohlson Group.

At our company, we know how to sell, service, market, teach, mentor, protect, and editorialize on this great business. We also answer the phone! We don't have a computerized menu for you to use so we can "save a few bucks." I don't like them and don't think you do either. We really care. We make money when you make money. We are also very financially literate. We can assist you in analyzing companies and products. I've even designed some of these products. I've been involved in all facets of the industry. Does this make me better? Not necessarily. Does this make me different? Absolutely. Does my staff share my passion and conviction for what we do? YOU BET YOUR LIFE THEY DO!! Is my staff incentivized and compensated based on your success? Just ask them: they win when you win!

So, that's how I came up with our slogan. It's very simple, very short, but, I think it says it all. Thanks to all of you who are experiencing "the difference!" If we are messing up, call us and tell us. Please! If you haven't done business with us, give us a try. I'm confident that you will say that working with The Ohlson Group IS "a different experience!"

Chapter 10

Fear

Fear is a powerful emotion. Some say that they are motivated by fear. Others simply shut down when the feeling sweeps over them. Fear is usually something that creeps over us without warning. Due to its swiftness, we often become paralyzed and don't know how to react. This inability to react can have devastating circumstances. The solution rests in identifying and understanding the cause of the fear—not an easy task but one that is possible.

I recently watched, for about the tenth time, the movie *Replacements* starring Keanu Reeves and Gene Hackman. Hackman, the coach of this rag tag group of NFL replacements, was doing all that he could to motivate his team after suffering a heartbreaking loss the previous Sunday. They now were facing a game that would determine if they made the playoffs. The coach felt as though there was a lack of trust among the teammates. He realized that most teams had months to learn to trust each other, but he knew he had but one week to get the players to believe in one another. So, he started to force a dialogue. Here's how it went:

The coach wrote the word FEAR on the board and asked the players to speak about their fears. After hearing about spiders and insects, Reeves' character finally said that he feared quicksand. The players asked him to explain. He stated that the quicksand feeling came about when one thing went wrong, and then another, and then another. You try fighting, but the quicksand takes you under. Without something to grab hold of or someone to help, you slide under the sand to a certain death! It's the same in business. Make sure you have a team you trust to pull you out.

With a helping hand—someone to reach out and give you support—you can crawl out of the muck and get onto solid ground. But, you have to *TRUST* that person to help you. We all have fears. We all dread the thought of stepping into the "quicksand" of business failure. No matter how successful we may have been, we know that it could all come crashing down on top of us if we aren't careful. To be honest, a small amount of fear is probably a good thing—it keeps us working, moving forward.

But irrational fear is crippling, and the solution, again, is trust. Trust in yourself, first. Know that you can and will succeed. Trust in your staff, know that they will support you if you give them the tools and training they need. And finally, trust the professionals with whom you work—the attorneys, the accountants, the advisors, and yes, the marketing organization, who will be there to help you—pull you out of the quicksand—as long as you extend a hand to them.

Chapter 11

Wax Paper Vision

Can you even imagine spending your day when your sight is as cloudy as wax paper? That's the way my mother described her vision prior to her cataract removal. Well, I'm lucky that I have great vision, from a medical perspective, and hope that you do to. But what about from a "non-medical" perspective? Let's take a "look".

Have you ever been in a personal or professional situation when things just don't seem to be clear? I know that I have. It's tough to peel that wax paper off and get a good look at what has happened and what's coming at you. Here's what sometimes may happen.

You wake up concerned and your mind is spinning. You have a problem (challenge) and nothing seems clear (wax paper). You begin your day with a pledge to yourself to focus on the situation and go home with a crystal clear image of the situation at hand and a sure-fire prescription for success. Sometimes it works, but more often than not, you may wake up tomorrow with the same blurry image. So, why is this happening? Here's my non-medical "diagnosis."

I feel that our normal lives come into play. We have to function, earn a living, take care of the kids, or deal with some other crucial issue. We are then lulled to sleep. Our vision seems much better because we are focusing on clearer objects. In other words, we have taken our "eye off the ball." So what's a person to do? Here's my mini-prescription to help get you on the road to good "visual" health:

- Wake up and write down the challenge.
- Don't kick yourself because you have to deal with other challenges/opportunities. That's just life!
- Before lunch, pull out the piece of paper with the challenge, close your door, shut off the phones, and spend fifteen minutes brainstorming on how you can remedy this illness.
- Set a timeline for improvement (not a permanent cure).
- Stay the course. As you move through life, new opportunities will expose themselves and many times will help you cure your original problem.

In other words: PLAN YOUR WORK AND WORK YOUR PLAN! We are only human. Don't look away. Stare right into that wax paper and don't settle for that blurry outlook on life. You deserve more! You will win and you will find yourself shaving or putting on your makeup singing that old song—"I can see clearly now."

Chapter 12

Independence with Affiliation

I love this phrase! You've probably heard it before. One of my previous carriers used this phrase quite often. I embraced it twenty years ago as a concept rather than a statement. I believe that today it is more relative to our business than ever before. So please bear with me if I happen to reference this message many times over the balance of the year. What exactly does "Independence with Affiliation" mean and how could it affect your business? Please allow me to explain.

Our industry is going through unbelievable changes. Many companies are struggling to stay in the game. There are many reasons for this. First, many companies' profits are being squeezed due to the low interest rate environment that we have been dealing with. These 45-year-low rates make it difficult for a company to make the profit spread that it needs to stay in the market. *(The spread is the difference between what the life insurance company earns on their investments subtracted by what they credit the policy-owner).* So, decisions are then made. They are, but not limited to, bringing crediting rates to minimums, reducing commissions, pulling the products, or selling the company. This morning's newspaper listed two old companies that were just acquired.

Ratings also play a big part in our business. The insurance companies are striving to "stay" in the "A" category with A.M. Best and to achieve similar rating with the other agencies. Hence, capital becomes an issue—"the more business a company writes, the more capital it needs." Write too much business and not acquire new capital, and your ratings go down. This concept of writing too much business is a hard concept for most to understand (call me if you would like to discuss it in detail). So, what am I leading up to and what does this have to do regarding "Independence with Affiliation"?

Okay, here's part of the answer. The agent, producer, planner, advisor, or whatever else we call ourselves needs to have a team leader. Needs a scout. Needs a beacon in the fog. Needs someone to be the observation deck and assist them in success. In other words, still be independent, but have a strong affiliation with an organization. I contend that the strongest affiliation should be with the marketing company and not with the life company. The marketing company's interests are aligned with yours. It is successful when you are successful. The life insurance company has other concerns and "other fish to fry."

In summary, I believe that the professionals who sell financial services will soon fall into two categories:

THE BROKER

Goes from marketing company to marketing company. Looks for the hot deal and the special commission and is not interested in a strong relationship. In other words, he or she will be a "customer" of the marketing organization not a client. I will always treat the broker with dignity and respect and look forward to earning his or her business. But, I believe that it will be more transaction oriented.

THE ASSOCIATE

This individual is looking for an organization that can always provide quality products, marketing concepts, strong compensation, operational assistance, and exceptional back office and top notch financial guidance when choosing a carrier. In other words, a STRATEGIC ALLIANCE—A RELATIONSHIP. A bond lasting long into the future. These are the people with whom we will walk in this century.

You see, we can hang by ourselves or we can hang together. INDEPENDENCE WITH AFFILIATION—more than a statement—a concept that guarantees mutual respect and a common goal!

Chapter 13

The Eight Minute Performance

My wife and I spent a weekend at Indiana University in Bloomington, Indiana. Our daughter, the youngest of our three children, was participating in "IU Sing." IU Sing is a big tradition with a long history of putting on quality musical productions. Here's what they do and how it works. First, a fraternity and a sorority are paired together. They are to develop an eight minute musical using the theme provided to them by the university. They write the script, write the music, develop a band, choreograph the production, get the costumes, and get ready to compete against thirty different acts. This program spreads over Friday and Saturday evening.

Well, there were about seventy people in my daughter's group! They rehearsed for five weeks! (This is a really big deal!) They probably had twenty hours per week in practice—that's over one hundred hours of preparation for this *eight minute performance!*

The acts were amazing. Some looked like Broadway shows. Their task was daunting. They had to accomplish the following:

- Immediately engage the audience.
- Get the audience to "like" them.
- Present themselves in a way that "explodes" in the audience's mind.
- Make sure that each part of the performance was perfectly timed.
- Build up to the crescendo.
- Perform their closing number.
- Ask for the audience's approval (their vote).

As I said, it was quite a daunting task. I couldn't help but relate their act to our business. We are trying to do the same thing in our sales presentation. We try to engage our prospect, build trust, perform along the way, provide an idea that explodes in their minds, close, and hope they buy.

Some of us have been doing this for so long that it has become old hat. But, I have a couple of questions for you—Are we spending enough time in "rehearsal?" Are we putting on our best performance? I remember someone telling me that "All business is show business."

Take a few minutes to review your script. Make sure you know when to sing and when to listen. Prepare the build-up and then provide the most convincing rationale for doing business with you. Don't delay. You won't have all day. Remember, it's just an *"Eight Minute Performance."*

Chapter 14

Cast Your Ballots!
It's Your Right
and Your Responsibility

Voting day across America is important for all of the obvious reasons, though, unfortunately, millions of eligible voters don't ever exercise this fundamental right. What an opportunity and privilege to be able to choose our representatives! Even though the national political races seem to gain most of the press coverage, in reality, our local races usually have a more direct effect on our lives.

America has changed dramatically since 9/11. People are more concerned and aware about all aspects of their lives. Personal time, freedom, financial security, national defense, family and friendship dominate our minds. Honesty and integrity are personal attributes that are attracting people in all forms of business and life in general. Perhaps because of 9/11, more young people are getting involved in the political process than before—taking time to learn about candidates and casting their votes.

Our clients are casting ballots every day. They cast a ballot when they choose to do business with us. They recognize qualities in us, such as honesty and integrity, as being important indicators of our "business character" and they choose or "vote" to let us handle their financial matters.

Just as voting requires a significant amount of personal responsibility, serving our clients requires at least as much responsibility. How do politicians know if they are doing the right things? How do we know if we are doing things right? I believe that there is only one way to know for sure. When you think about what to do for your clients each day—and I hope you DO think about it each day—consider the message in this simple poem that I read a couple of times a year. It reveals a simple life lesson that applies to each of us as Americans, as financial services professionals, as human beings. I hope that you enjoy it as much as I do, and I hope you win your clients' "votes" because you live by its lesson.

THE MAN IN THE GLASS

When you get what you want in your struggle for self
And the world makes you king for a day,
Just go to a mirror and look at yourself
And see what THAT man has to say.

For it isn't your father, mother, or wife
Whose judgment upon you must pass;
The fellow whose verdict counts most in your life
Is the one staring back from the glass.

Some people may think you a straight-shootin' chum
And call you a wonderful guy,
But the man in the glass says you're only a bum—
If you can't look him straight in the eye.

He's the fellow to please—never mind all the rest,
For he's with you clear up to the end.
And you've passed your most dangerous, difficult test
If the man in the glass is your friend.

You may fool the whole world down the pathway of life
And get pats on your back as you pass.
But your final reward will be heartaches and tears—
If you've cheated the man in the glass!

~ Author Unknown ~

See you at the polls!

Chapter 15

Agent Satisfaction

I recently read the results of a National Customer Loyalty Study by Indianapolis-based *Walker Information*. The focus of their study is on the retail segment, but I noticed a great deal of similarity with the financial services sector. Reading this study came at a very important time for me as we were fine-tuning our marketing plan for the coming year and beyond. As an Insurance Marketing Organization (IMO), we are faced with the same dilemma: how to ensure agent satisfaction and, most important, AGENT LOYALTY."

We are able to provide better service if we are dealing with a loyal group of agents and financial planners. We are then spending the vast majority of our time servicing that group as opposed to "the shopper." This perspective or mindset proves to be more profitable for all involved. You, the agent, get better information and support, the client gets a better package due to the research involved in the planning process and we, the IMO, are not spending an inordinate amount of time, money, and manpower looking for new producers. So, how do we propose to accomplish this feat?

Here's what we do:

- We are agent focused. Unlike many home offices, we understand that "The Agent is King (or Queen)" in our organization. <u>You</u> are our most valuable asset. Our entire staff believes in this statement. Each staff member has a marketing background, each understands the challenges of your profession, and each is "incentivized." They know that if you are successful, The Ohlson Group is successful, and I reward the entire team!
- Our reputation is strong. People who have dealt with me over the last thirty years know that my word is my bond. It is not a cliché; I mean it! This doesn't mean we don't ever make mistakes; on rare occasions, we do. But, we admit to them; we apologize, and we fix the problem. WE ARE ON <u>YOUR</u> TEAM!
- Quality products—I use my experience as a former president of

a major life insurance company to achieve this goal. I've developed and priced products, and I understand a company's financials. We represent the financially strong!

- "The Shopping Experience." Sound crazy? I disagree. You, as the planner, are in situations many times in which you are looking for a unique product or service. We make it easy for you to find what you want. A technical question? If we don't have the answer, we will get it for you—and I mean QUICKLY!

- Professional and knowledgeable staff—our people are trained on all product lines we offer. We are not a big "spreadsheet company" that represents 100 companies and offers 400 plans. You can't be knowledgeable on that many and you don't need that many. We also develop a better home office relationship when we are more focused. We are many times able to get policies issued more quickly, get an underwriting concession, and receive a better reception when requesting a special service request. PLUS, we have a wide enough portfolio to service and support the loyal associate.

- Information: this is where we excel. Our Ohlson Report, special e-mail notifications, our website www.ohlsongroup.com, *For Members Only* section, teleconferences, archived meetings, CE meetings, local and regional sales meetings, and special consultants to our organization insure you the news, when it's news on a 24/7 basis!

I'm sure that you are fine-tuning your marketing plan and that you desire to achieve greater client loyalty. I hope that our approach to enhance agent loyalty will be helpful in your practice. I know that you can shop anywhere for your financial services products and services. Please allow me to be this bold: "Our products, commissions, and services are as good as any…and better than most." But, we will work our "you know what" off to earn and keep your business.

Thanks to all of you who do business with us. For you, I ask for an opportunity to earn your loyalty. For those of you investigating The Ohlson Group, I ask for the opportunity to earn your first piece of business. I'm confident that you will understand why we say that dealing with The Ohlson Group is…*a different experience*!

Chapter 16

What Happened?

Near the end of 2004, all three markets were roaring towards the finish line. The Dow was up, NASDAQ was up, and Standard & Poor was up. Interest rate increases were supposed to be moderate by the Feds. Inflation appeared tame. Housing starts were strong and looked to continue the upward trend. Everybody was happy. The new year—2005—looked promising!

However, as 2005 unfolded, we saw dramatic changes: one day, the Dow closed down 98 points and the Fed revealed it was concerned about inflation and that interest rate increases would be swifter and more severe. We were also told that housing starts would slow and that bond yields would go up with bond prices going down. What happened? At the end of 2004, everything looked rosy.

Well, in 2005, nothing really new happened. It was just "life" as we have come to know it—ever changing, always challenging! Have we not witnessed market meltdowns in the past? Haven't we said before that interest rates have been at historic lows? And while we are on the subject, a little inflation isn't always bad. Likewise, if 30-year fixed interest rates go to 7%, it will still be a relatively good deal. The question your clients are always asking is not "*what* happened," but rather, "what shall we do *now?*"

No matter what kind of year we are living through—good or bad—the first thing we need to do, as financial services professionals, is communicate with our clients. Calm their fears. Review their present programs. Consider, perhaps, rebalancing or reallocating. During tough times, it might be a great time to show your clients how a 98 point drop in the Dow, for example, did not create a loss!

This is your time to shine. This is when the life and annuity sales person sizzles—in a *hot* market. Remember, we <u>don't sell *hot* products</u>, <u>we sell *safe* products</u>. This is the time to shout it from the mountain tops. Use it in your seminars or write your clients a letter. Do anything you can to communicate your message to your clients.

I'm more excited today than last week. This is what we are trained to do. I don't focus on what happened, but rather, I work on what will happen when we stay in touch with our clients and stay on top of the solid information that will help them ride out any storm that appears!

Chapter 17

Two Minute Warning!

We are all familiar with the final two minutes of play in sporting events such as football and basketball. Football's two minute offense has always intrigued me. A team, that hasn't moved the ball in the entire quarter, puts together a drive and scores with a little time on the clock. They utilize every available resource. They use the sidelines to stop the clock. They may use a "no-huddle" offense to take advantage of remaining ticks on the clock. They may intentionally spike the ball to salvage extra time. The time outs are used at the most opportune times. The good teams know that the game may be won at the end. In other words, the way you finish is just as important as the way you begin. I believe that it's the same way in business.

I view the entire month of December as my "two minute drill." It's not only important to continue to work hard and keep scoring, but to prepare for the next game. The next game in my mind is next year. The way I finish will have a significant impact and prove to be an indicator as to how I will compete next year.

It's very easy to shut down and coast at the end of the game (year).

Recently, my alma mater blew a 15-point lead and lost their basketball game in an upset. They were playing "not to lose" as opposed to insuring a win. A bad finish can carry over to the next game (year) and affect one's future record (income). The well prepared team (financial services professional) knows how to finish. He/she is trained properly and is ready for any, and all, contingencies.

So teammates, the clock has warned us, the announcer has just said "two minutes," and we have to muster up some additional energy and finish strong. Here are some suggestions:

1) Analyze the year to date. Look at both successes and failures (missed shots). Were they good looks that didn't go in or bad shots? Analyze your mistakes only to the point where it can increase the possibility for future wins.

2) Write down your goals. All of them—both personal and professional.

3) Look at the resources that you have to make these goals a reality. Time, money and manpower.

4) Refine and reduce your lists to "Must do's" and "Nice to do's".

5) Reduce to writing.

6) Put together a timeline for completion.

7) Determine who your teammates will be (companies, distributors, other professionals, etc.)

8) Make sure each goal is backed up with a marketing plan—not a sales plan. You need the marketing plan that will allow you to fill the stadium with spectators (qualified prospects).

9) Give copies of your plan to all involved.

10) Commit!

11) Enjoy the rest of the game (year).

You will enjoy the post game and be refreshed for the next kick-off or tip-off. You are probably already a winner. A little more planning and preparation may get you next year's championship.

Chapter 18

Terroir

I enjoy the taste of a nice wine. It brings out the best in a fine meal, it encourages relaxation and conversation with friends, and it can give us great life lessons. You may be asking yourself, "how can wine give us a life lesson?" Well, here's the word of the day—*Terroir.*

There is no single word in English that can adequately convey this all-important French concept. When the French use this one word, they mean the "sum total of every environmental influence on a vineyard—from the number of sunshine hours it experiences, to the kind of soil it's made up of, to how often it's rained on." For the French, the ultimate smell, texture, and taste of any great wine is dependent more on the *terroir* of the vineyard from which it came than on the skill of the person who made the wine.

A wine collector and good friend who enjoys studying all aspects of wine first explained this word to me. After listening, I felt as though *terroir* pertains to all of us. It is the sum total of every environmental influence on our lives (vineyard). It's the circumstances by which we were raised, the hardships we've gone through, and the great victories we've experienced.

Our children get a lot of our *terroir*. They watch what we do (actions speak louder than words), listen to what we say, and, many times, emulate our lives. They, like us, experience sunshine and rain on their vineyards. We often try to keep an umbrella over them for protection. However, each of us has had rain and sunshine in our lives—to make us stronger and wiser—to make us who we are today.

Now, what does any of this have to do with the retirement planning business?

1) The more we know about our clients "terroir" the more successful we will be in dealing with them.
2) You, the producer, come from great "terroir". It takes a unique person to be successful in our business. So be proud.

When I was hiring salespeople, I have always felt that their attitude was, in most cases, more important that their aptitude. Just as the French say, *"the taste of any great wine is dependent more on the terroir of the vineyard from which it came than on the skill of the person who made the wine."*

Part II

The Senior Market

Chapter 19

It's A Puzzle!

Working with seniors' financial situation is like putting a puzzle together. There are many different pieces. The puzzle is not completed until the last piece has been put into position. Only then, does the picture truly come to life and make sense. Let me take you back in time.

Remember when you worked with puzzles as a child? Maybe you've done puzzles with your kids or grandkids? The big pieces were always easy, right? Maybe it was the dog's face and nose that came together and allowed you to rapidly put pieces together. The puzzle started to come to life, and before long, the entire dog's body appeared. But, what if the image didn't come into view? What if you walked away in frustration? One solution was calling for help. Sometimes, the extra pair of eyes helps to complete this endeavor.

The puzzle is an example as to the way many advisors work the Senior Market. Some just go for the easy pieces (sales) and then leave the table. The client then has to call someone else for assistance to complete the puzzle (the financial plan). Problem is that we have allowed another advisor to complete the puzzle (plan). Not unlike the puzzle example, the person who finishes it is the hero. The person who did the easy work (made the easy sale) is not held in as high regard as the advisor who finished the exercise. How can today's professional advisor in the senior market ensure he is the one to fit the final pieces into the puzzle? Let's take a look.

First, it's of utmost importance that the advisor ask questions. These questions should be more structured than just a casual discussion. The advisor should come armed with a professional financial questionnaire. This questionnaire, or fact finder, should discover the following:

1) What are their assets?
2) When did they purchase these assets?
3) Why did they purchase?
4) What do they have planned (uses) for these dollars?
5) Are they happy with their purchase?
6) If yes, "Why?" If not, "Why not?"

Second, you must examine the client's risk tolerance. For example, are they risk-takers, risk-averse, or ultra-conservative? Have them take a quiz. Then, analyze the outcome. For example, if they are ultra-conservative, why do they have the majority of their money at risk?

Third, explore their dreams for the future. It doesn't matter if they are eighty years old—they still have dreams. These dreams may not be for them. They may be for their children, grandkids, charities, or other institutions. They may have close ties to their religious organizations.

Fourth, ask what their greatest concerns are. Have them write down their concerns in the order of importance. Then, ask them to establish a timeline for completion.

Fifth, make an initial recommendation based upon their responses, or set an appointment for a follow-up implementation meeting. When the sale is completed, make sure they understand that planning is an ongoing process and this is just the initial step toward the realization of their goals. You will be back for reviews and will always be at their disposal. Let them know that you don't have all of the answers, but you have access to all of the solutions.

My point is that planning with seniors is complicated. There are many pieces to their financial puzzle. No one expects you to know all of the answers. But, they do expect you to be able to *find* the answers. That's why I continually stress the importance of strategic alliances with other professionals. You should be the quarterback of the team, conductor of the symphony, and the finisher of the puzzle.

Don't leave the door open for someone else to make additional sales and take over the role of quarterback. You made the first sale; now complete the puzzle. You will be held in high esteem, make additional income, and generate many referrals. It's really not that *puzzling*.

Chapter 20

Hurricane Protection

My heart, thoughts, and prayers went out to our business associates and friends in the Southeast United States during that terrible time when four major hurricanes struck the region in the summer and fall of 2004. What an awful time they are having! The people will be feeling the economic impact of these storms for years to come. The storms also had a significant impact on our business. However, these kinds of tragedies can help us explain, through simple analogies, how important our work is in the real world—we offer "hurricane protection" from life's unexpected storms.

On the negative side, many of our associates had to move out of their homes and offices. Seminars have been cancelled. Money invested in the mailings has been flushed down the proverbial toilet. The last thing that senior prospects wanted to think about during the chaos of the storms and the recovery period immediately following was reviewing their retirement situation. Many were frightened, concerned, overwhelmed, and glued to the weather channel. They were not racing to their cell phones to call us for an appointment!

On the positive side, however, most will see the insurance industry at its best. Sure, it will be primarily the property and casualty side, but they will step up to the plate. The insurance premiums will provide dollars to rebuild clients' lives. The disaster also brought a stark reality to people's minds. Planning for the future, regardless of your age, is of great importance.

Now please don't misunderstand my motive here: I'm not suggesting that we financial services professionals take advantage and play on our prospects' heartstrings or use scare tactics during times of local, regional, or national tragedies. We all know that major storms, like life itself, take many very unexpected turns and that we (including us) need to plan for these emergencies. This is the lesson of the Florida hurricanes in 2004.

The winds will die down. The seas will calm and Florida will once again be the Sunshine State we have all learned to love, admire, and sometimes envy. So you should use these events, in a most professional way, to <u>remind</u> your clients that there is always a tropical disturbance lingering somewhere out at sea. Use the simple storm analogy:

"We never know how storms will develop, but we usually get warnings from the hurricane center telling us to prepare. In most cases, we will have time to secure our families, homes, and businesses from destruction—but sometimes the warnings come too late!"

Then move to the other real life issues that may rise up like a sudden storm:

"Not so with health issues, nursing home stays, critical illness, or death. We all need to make sure that we have our "financial homes" in order—prepared for any emergency."

Plywood can't help your clients with the above-mentioned financial hazards, but we professional financial services advisors can!

Chapter 21

"It's Just What We Were Looking For!"

Isn't that what you long to hear from your prospects? The sale is made, the prospect is happy, and referrals are plentiful. Doesn't seem to happen that often, does it? What's the secret? And, who runs an operation that makes people react in this fashion?

Let's take a look at the tale of two companies. Let's first examine the venerable, and often admired, Marshall Fields. Marshall Fields always makes fond memories spring to life in my mind. I was born in Chicago and went with my parents on the annual Christmas pilgrimage to visit Santa at Marshall Fields on State Street. What a store!! Still is today. You always know what to expect at this establishment. Not a lot of surprises, but always quality and great tradition.

Unfortunately, Marshall Fields is not doing all that well today. They've had some disappointing earnings and sales. Their parent, Target Stores, is seriously thinking about putting it up for sale. Hard to imagine.

Now consider another retailer—Stein Mart. This operation makes money and has loyal, repeat customers. The true Stein Mart "groupie" makes several visits per month. Why do they do this?

"Stein Mart is an experience!" they say. They always bring in new and different merchandise. They display it in sections. Sometimes in stacks. You can get everything from clothing to furnishings to accessories. People seem to buy things that they never planned to buy, things they weren't even thinking about! But, when they see them, they say, "It's just what we were looking for!"

You see, the dishes are near the color coordinated placemats, that are in close proximity to the unique outdoor drinking glasses, that are right around the corner from the wine glasses, that are displayed with the wine stoppers! Great merchandising! It's as if they are not selling merchandise; rather, they are <u>SELLING BENEFITS</u>! (Hey! That's one of *our* terms!)

Stein Mart is selling the fun that you will have with your patio dishware. How can you purchase these without the wine glasses? Oh, and you'll also <u>need</u> the clear wine cooler to keep your wine chilled on that beautiful side table you just purchased here.

Now, what do we, financial services professionals, have to do to make people feel this good about our merchandise? We have to SELL BENEFITS—not features. Here's a cold, hard fact: <u>all</u> insurance companies and agents have products with features. They are just like the department stores. But, here's the crucial difference. The good agent:

1) asks the right questions,
2) determines the need and desire of the prospect,
3) strolls the prospect down the "aisle of life,"
4) gets them to acknowledge that they have a void in their financial plan, and
5) presents the solution in a manner that explodes in the prospect's mind.

It's the Stein Mart effect applied to <u>our</u> business!

Maybe we need to re-examine the way we explain our products. How about:

- a fixed index annuity versus an equity index annuity?
- tax advantaged wealth transfer versus single premium life insurance?
- a "<u>LIVING MEMORIAL</u>" *free of federal income tax* versus a <u>TAX FREE DEATH BENEFIT</u>?

Just a few thoughts. All department stores have a Santa at Christmas. They will always be around, but the competition is fierce. Tell stories, engage the prospect, talk about their dreams, and provide them with the product that produces the desired benefit. You will have a better chance at making the sale and might even hear them say, "You're just who we've been looking for!"

Chapter 22

"The Times, They Are A-Changin'!"

Nearly everyone who hails from the Baby Boomer generation remembers those Dylan words sung during our "Woodstock Days." Many songs of the day spoke to the societal changes that America was undergoing: Well, "the times are a-changin'" again, my friends! I am referring to our financial services industry. I am specifically addressing the Senior Market. Let's take a look.

I have had the opportunity to meet with many top senior executives of some of our major life insurance companies. I have also had the opportunity to speak with presidents on down, via the telephone, regarding challenges facing our industry. Capital issues and range wars for distribution are still high on their list of concerns. But, the issue of "suitability" in the Senior Market looms over the heads of insurance companies and producers alike. Some view this as an obstacle. I view it as an opportunity <u>and</u> a responsibility. Let me explain:

Effective September 1, 2004, Senior Suitability Requirements took effect in California, Arizona, and some other states. The purpose was to make sure that seniors purchasing financial products, annuities, and life insurance, in particular, are buying products that <u>they need</u> with a product design that is suitable for their current situation. Really, what's wrong with the "spirit" of the concept? We can all find fault in "the letter" of the law. I predict that the professional financial planner will find even greater rewards. The "slam bam….thank you ma'am" guys will go on to some other venture. We, as pros, will just need to adjust our sales and marketing programs. We might as well get started, because the baby boomers will soon be our prospects. They will come armed with more information and the products will be more "consumer-friendly". Oh, that's happening already? Okay, here are my predictions:

1) Products that are being offered today with mega surrender periods and charges that will choke a horse will cease to exist. *(I predict that one of America's top selling products will be gone in 30–60 days!)*

2) Insurance departments will not approve products that have over 10 years of surrender to any consumer age 71 and above. *(Double digit charges will see the same fate as the debit policy)*.
3) Regulators will find the agent guilty until proven innocent. *(Ready, shoot, aim)*.
4) Products will be more competitive.
5) Commissions will reduce
6) AND WE WILL MAKE MORE MONEY!!!

HOW? Competition will decrease. We good guys will control the market. We will start the "total development" of our client base (cross selling), and clients will seek us out. Sound like a mystery novel? I've been fortunate to have been on both sides of the house (home office and field). I believe I know what's going to happen. I'm confident that I can lead good producers to the promise land. The times are indeed "a-changin'—are you ready to adjust to the new world?

Chapter 23

"Dance To The Music!"

Remember that old song, "Dance To The Music," by Sly and The Family Stone? If you do, you are near my age. That song was blaring from dorms, fraternity and sorority houses, and car radios during the 1960s and 70s. Thankfully, we still hear it today. The beat, the harmony, and the driving bass make you want to get up out of your seat and dance! It can make you feel alive.

That's the great thing about music. There is a type for every mood and occasion. Music has also allowed people to express themselves. We can link types of music, even specific songs, to events that changed our country as well as events that changed our individual lives. Music has always been, is, and will always be important, therefore, in all of our lives. Is there a lesson in this (music) that we can apply to our business lives? Let's think about it!

I went to Chicago with my wife and our best friends. We were celebrating Valentine's Day and our friend's birthday. We had a great time. Being a frustrated former (and current) musician, I led my entourage to a number of music venues. We thoroughly enjoyed ourselves (I hope I speak for the whole group!) We heard rock, soul, jazz, and Chicago Blues. What I noticed most, however, was a common thread through all of these performances. Each group of musicians performed, sometime during their act, a musical "standard." Let me define what I mean by a musical standard

"Standards" are songs that have stood the test of time. They are songs that artists around the world re-record (or "cover" as they now say). They are also songs that artists can also improvise and play in another musical style than the original version. We usually associate Frank Sinatra, Tony Bennett, Bobby Darin, Dean Martin, Mel Tormé, Jerry Vale, and Louie Armstrong with these standards in music, as composers and/or performers. But there are so many other men and women who "qualify" as creators or performers of standards.

The Beatles wrote songs that are now becoming "standards." For example, whether you like it or not, how many different versions of McCartney's "Yesterday" have you heard? How many pop hits from the 1960s, 70s, 80s, and even 90s are now the soundtracks behind well-known TV or radio commercials?

I purchased Steve Tyrell's and Rod Stewart's new albums for my wife as Valentine gifts. Both are CDs of "standards." Stewart's album is his second of this type! They have been his biggest hits in number of album sales. Steve Tyrell is great. You might remember him from singing the closing song, "Just the Way You Look Tonight," in the hit movie, "Father of the Bride." Well, we sang all the way home from our Chicago trip. We had a great time! The songs we had just enjoyed, again, were comforting and safe. They made us feel good! Get ready for a leap to our business world!

Are you playing the "standards" for your clients? Or, are you just playing the newest, catchy tune (product)—something that is "here today and gone tomorrow?" Please don't misunderstand me. I think that Rap, Hip-Hop, Punk, and other types of "modern music" are worthwhile forms of art. But, most of these songs won't stand the test of time. I know that's a bold statement, but I believe it. Can you imagine hearing "Who Let The Dogs Out" blasting on an elevator in 2015 or so?

Our senior clients remember the "standards" as well. They like the comfortable, secure, and happy feeling they get when listening. They understand them; they enjoy them; they react positively to them. So, "play those hits" that will live forever…it's time to *pull those old records off the shelf.*"

I'm talking about these hits of our business:

- Guarantees
- Tax Deferred Growth on Annuities and Life
- Tax Free Death Benefit
- Safety
- Probate Free
- Payable to a Named Beneficiary
- Rates that historically outpace inflation
- Peace of Mind
- A Living Legacy (memorial)
- Liquidity

- And, AN INCOME THEY CANNOT OUTLIVE!!

WOW! Those are catchy tunes. They've been around forever. Our clients are still buying and requesting them! And, they will still be buying them long after you and I have retired. By the way, at the Ohlson Group, we have all these great tunes in stock! So, give one of our "music experts" a call and we will assist you in picking out the perfect "number" for your client.

Chapter 24

Sit Back And Enjoy The Ride

I was waiting at the airport for two of my associates to arrive. Their plane from Minneapolis had been delayed due to bad weather. It turned out that I would have an hour to cool my heels. Fortunately, I was mentored properly as a young salesman, and I always try to use my down time to jot down some notes, review the past few days, and take a look at my up and coming schedule. I was about ready to get out of my car and walk in the airport when I heard Paul Harvey on the radio deliver some interesting facts. He really caught my attention.

Mr. Harvey started by stating that the Mercury Grand Marquis and the Ford Crown Victoria were the most purchased cars by cab companies and the most favored by cab drivers. The styles of these cars have changed very little since 1995 and there are no major alterations planned for the next couple of years. Guess who else purchased these two car models? The answer isn't too surprising—Americans over age 65. When surveyed, these older Americans reported that these models are:

- a good value,
- very spacious with nothing fancy,
- have great passenger room for the grandkids,
- have plenty of power,
- are trustworthy, and
- have strong name brand.

Because these Seniors are also repeating customers, the manufacturers can keep their advertising and marketing cost lower. The Seniors said that they re-purchase because:

- It's easy,
- It's what they know,
- They are comfortable with the product,
- The purchasing process involves little or no stress, and
- Decision making is easy.

The good car salesman understands these facts. They are not selling features such as—a Bose sound system, 16 speakers, 8-way seats, power folding rear seat, or optional 4-wheel drive. The good salesman sells and promotes the benefits the Seniors want and need. What does all of this mean to us in the financial services business in the Senior Market? Simply this: you should market the following benefits to Seniors

- safety,
- security,
- good for family and grandkids,
- no fancy frills,
- easy to purchase,
- good brand name,
- power (EIAs),
- a very good value, and
- no stress.

I believe that we will all do better if we find out what the Senior *really* wants. Let's not impose our values on them. They know what they want. They are just waiting for someone to ask them!

Chapter 25

Federal Oversight

We have had a very exciting and profitable run in the life insurance business. I include annuities and all *fixed* products for the purposes of this book. Agents and insurance companies alike have been able to do just about what they've wanted to do without the *Feds* looking over their shoulder. Our business has been governed by each state insurance department.

Each department has its own rules, forms, and solvency requirements. They even have different licensing, suitability, and continuing education standards. There have been simplifications through which a number of state insurance commissioners have adopted similar requirements. But, there is a long way to go. I believe that there will be national licensing, national continuing education standards, and national suitability and compliance guidelines. This will significantly reduce the costs for state governments and simplify the process for all involved. However, I believe that attempting to get all fifty states to agree on anything is a monumental and time-consuming task. Plus, I don't believe we have the time.

The insurance companies have released products that they thought would give them significant distribution and penetration. The products were designed based upon necessary company profits and the *perceived* commission requirements of the producer. I would love to say that the policyholder was number one on the list of considerations, but I can't. I believe that the companies believed that we could sell anything. And, for the most part, we did.

Well, the Federal Government has been kicking the *you-know-what* out of the mutual fund business. And, for good reason. I say this being a proud holder of a Series 7 for longer than many of you have been in the business. The property and casualty industry has taken it on the chin for *bid-rigging*.

This is now bringing about a full disclosure of commission environment for that segment of the insurance business. Trust Mills are being exposed and punished. Agents, unlicensed for securities, are being prosecuted for selling registered products. California, through Senate Bill 620, has established some of the most stringent guidelines on agents marketing to the age 65 and above marketplace. I believe that this is just the beginning of the crackdown. The *California model* will find its way from the Pacific to the Atlantic. So, what does that mean for all of us?

The vast majority of agents will be just fine. We've been doing things the right way forever. We put our clients' needs first. We believe that selling the proper product to satisfy our client's needs will result in great profitability for the professional advisor. The *"my commission first"* mentality will wither and die, soon, I hope. I also believe that the insurance companies are going to change the play book and take this concern away from us. Here's why:

The life insurance companies are well aware of current, as well as proposed, suitability and compliance guidelines. They will start developing products that truly put the consumer first. Don't get me wrong, many fine companies are already doing this.

Products will be simpler. They will have increased liquidity. Most will cease being *trust me* products in which the carrier can do whatever it wants with renewal crediting rates.

In other words, the business is going to take a step backward to make great strides in going forward. They will look back at history and embrace the principles that made this great industry what it is today. We are going to see products that we would sell to out parents (those products are out there with many fine companies). They will be pressed to publish renewal rates with regards to annuities. Guarantees will be longer. Upside for your client will be great. Policies will be easier to explain. And, you the professional advisor will make more money than you have ever imagined. We will once again concentrate on solving America's two greatest concerns:

1) the fear of dying too soon, and
2) the fear of living too long.

I've been on both sides of the table. As president of an insurance company, we were always concerned about distribution and what we needed to do to get business. As a board member of a publicly held company, I was always concerned with quarterly profitability. I like where I'm at today. I have the freedom to offer products through carriers that take care of all parties—the customer, the agent, and the insurance company. A fair deal for all us.

Federal oversight is a real possibility. I believe that we should examine what we are selling and ask the following question:

"Am I selling a product that I would feel comfortable having a regulator review?"

Why? Because they are coming to do just that!

Remember: SERVICE, CREDIBIILTY, INTEGRITY & PROFITABILITY (SCIP™). These are the cornerstones upon which I've built and will continue to build my business. Using this acronym as a guide will assure you the level of financial success that you deserve.

Chapter 26

Call Me Simple

We in the annuity business are truly in a unique position. We offer security, peace of mind and a "square" deal. But we are only human. We sometimes make things more difficult than they should be.

We often confuse the issues with our clients/prospects. We come prepared with fancy illustrations, complex tax ideas and sophisticated concepts for our clients when, in most cases, we could make the sale more quickly if we only gave them what they want.

How do we know what they want? Well, we must of course ask them! This "Greatest Generation" has been through it all: wars, the depression, recessions, rising pharmaceutical costs, world terror, and much more. These are the same people who are patriotic and proud of our country *and* their accomplishments. These are people who want simplicity, peace of mind and comfort. They are conditioned to spot the "too good to be true" deal. They buy from you only if they trust you. Chances are you are going to make the sale. So how do we break the ice in the initial conversation? How about starting with some good news?

Stories abound in the press about the strength of the human spirit. Look for them; they are there every day. Find them and make a mental note. Or, how about the fact that many of us feel as though the stock market has bottomed out and we are on our way up? How about reminding your prospects that most businesses are honest and straight-forward organizations. In short, be positive. Remind your customers that everything is going to be okay. Although this country has been through the ringer, we are doing pretty well, and it's going to get better. Sharing your positive vision, if only briefly, not only helps break the ice, but also shows that you are a positive person—a "glass is half full" person.

I then suggest you begin with a simple explanation of the benefits of an annuity. It's a pretty simple product that produces world-class results. Your annuity customers worry a lot. It's their job to worry. They worry about kids, grandkids, the world and their way of life. Cheer them up!! Be their friend; give them a fair deal, and everyone walks away feeling good about the meeting and good about life in general.

Ladies and gentlemen, we are now in the greatest decade for fixed annuities. Let's take advantage of the time. Everyone wins—you, your clients, our company and yes, even America! It's a simple but important message. Spread the word!

Chapter 27

Don't Worry…Be Happy!

It's hard to read a newspaper, watch the evening news, or read a news magazine without worrying. Believe me, I'm not dismissing the fact that there are events and happenings that should concern us greatly. The global economy, the "War on Terrorism," conflicts abroad, and the future happiness of our children are all issues we should take seriously.

I do believe that it is important for all of us to find the bright spots. I believe that they are plentiful. Concentrating on happiness and security can be tough when tragedy abounds. But, I believe that life will improve for all of us. I also believe that it can bring "happiness" to your clients and prospects. Allow me to explain.

We, as a people (particularly Americans), are eternal optimists. We all want to see the light at the end of the tunnel and want to feel good about life. (I was born in Chicago and still think that the Cubs may win it all this year!) People want to associate with people who are "up" and positive. Too many times, we are surrounded by "downers" and it's easy to fall in the hole with them. Unhappiness and a sense of defeat can lead to depression and a feeling of "what's the use." Some of your clients and prospects feel that way too. Let's look at how we can help them and make all of us feel like champs.

Your senior clients read the same newspapers you do. Many of them equate *security* with *happiness*. They have read about "scams" against seniors. They worked hard for their money and don't want to lose it. They've had promises broken and are looking for John Wayne—the hero riding in to save the day! So, fellow professionals, don your cowboy hat and get ready to ride! Remember the "Duke" and how he operated:

- Straight talk regarding what we offer (e.g., annuities).
- Don't sell it as a commodity. Sell all of the benefits (tax-deferred freedom from probate, lifetime income, etc.).
- Promise them superior service.

- Make their experience as good as the promise.
- Be ready to serve on demand.

In summary, let them know that today's annuities are flexible, safe, and can be customized to their needs. No, they don't have to contact a call center for information—they have you—professional, courteous, knowledgeable, and ready to listen…a lot like John Wayne. Help your senior clients feel secure and watch the happiness set in. Your clients know, from experience, that:

1) things could be a lot worse,
2) life is pretty great as it is, and
3) things will pass with time and life will only get better.

"The little reed, bending to the force of the wind, soon stood upright again when the storm had passed over."

—AESOP

Chapter 28

Deficit Spending

Have you ever heard the term "deficit spending?" "Daily," you say? You're probably right. The press seems to hammer on it almost daily, particularly during election years and when Congress is promoting some big budget bill. But, is deficit spending always bad? Now, I'm not really beginning a political discussion here. However, I am proposing what I call "good" deficit spending as we look ahead to each new quarter or new year. A definition or at least an explanation here:

In my view, "good" deficit spending is an investment that will reap a profitable return. It will help grow an organization or an entity. Today, we are facing challenges to our businesses. We have "do not call lists," anti-spam legislation, anti-faxing rules, and other new state laws that threaten to change the way we do business. However, these challenges can also bring about great opportunities. We must invest in new methods of marketing that may, and I emphasize *may*, turn into tremendous opportunities. We have to invest in ourselves. Financial service representatives who do so will, in time, reap greater market share. But, there must be experimentation. There must be some risk taking. There may even be times when you risk your capital, or borrow money, to try these new ventures. Hence, my view of "good" deficit spending. We spend money we've earmarked for other uses in a new, trial-and-error enterprise.

Here are some examples:

1. Put aside some money for a **new direct-mail program**. Be straightforward in your approach (no hooks, tell them you are selling an annuity or simplified issue life) so you get qualified prospects responding.
2. Try something that will **appeal to** the consumer **mass media**. What about newspaper, television, or radio? What about a regular column or radio show?
3. Develop or **redesign your** website. It's your **electronic brochure**. More and more seniors are going to the web to check

you out. What are they seeing? Are you putting your best foot forward?

4. Sponsor **client appreciation** coffees, luncheons, dinners, or even wine tastings. Admission charge? Ask them to bring another couple. Give a short presentation on a general topic that should be of interest and ask them to fill out an interest form to determine future topics, and then contact the viable prospects.
5. Advertise on senior websites.
6. Give a presentation at a senior organization's regularly sponsored meeting. Bring in the coffee and cookies.
7. Think about hiring a resource concierge. This person will be available to assist your clients in "non-product and non-planning" situations. In other words, be the source directing clients to all the information they need.
8. Write or purchase a **newsletter** to send to your current clients and prospects. Place your picture and biography on the piece and watch how you are perceived to be the expert in your area.

WHEW! And this is just a short list.

Where do you get the money for this if you don't have the money? How about borrowing? Would that be deficit spending? You betcha! But, it's good deficit spending. It will produce revenues that will pay off the loans, allow you to hire, expand, and prosper. Business and governments do this everyday. Did you ever have a student loan? Why? Because the degree put you in a position to earn more money and be more successful. Students continue to participate in this form of positive or "good" deficit spending today, and it's worth every penny!

Now, before you get out your checkbooks, look at your marketing/business plan. Here are some marketing plan components you should analyze:

- **Market Review**—Trends Overview, Market Segments, Target Market (both primary & secondary),
- **Product Review**—What will you present? Annuities, Single Premium Life, LTC, Med Supp, etc.
- **Look at strengths, weaknesses, opportunities and threats.**
- **Determine Sales Goals and Marketing Objectives.**
- **Develop Strategies For Positioning your products & services**—Communications and Promotions

- **Create An Action Plan and Implementation**—Media Plan, Budget, Schedule
- **Develop How To Evaluate Results**—Lead Tracking and Sales Reviews

So, how will you do next quarter, next year? You must keep growing. You do need to take risks, but make them calculated risks. Determine which ideas fit your business and dive in. Spend or borrow. Invest in yourself. Your clients believe in you, so believe in yourself! Practice GOOD deficit spending.

Chapter 29

Trilogy

Webster's defines trilogy as: "a series of three dramas or literary works or sometimes three musical compositions that are closely related and develop a single theme."

In our company, we have been working with a concept that we refer to as "trilogy." It is comprised of three elements:

1) A Single Premium Immediate Annuity (SPIA)
2) A Deferred Annuity
3) A Single Premium Life

Our goal is to address three of the most important concerns facing today's senior citizens.

- DISTRIBUTION: maintaining an income that will keep them in the world to which they have become accustomed (SPIA).
- ACCUMULATION: parking their money in a vehicle that gives them safety of principal, access to cash in the event of emergencies or opportunities, a rate of return that gives them the opportunity to outpace inflation and an additional distribution vehicle if money is required in the future (SPDA or FPDA).
- ESTATE PLANNING: a thoughtful and tax efficient means of passing down assets to named beneficiaries. These may be family (children or grandkids), charities, universities, service organizations or religious organizations. They desire a tax-free, probate-free and confidential means of handling this transaction (SPDA or FPDA).

How do we determine the amount that should be placed in each of these three compartments? The answer—a solid and thorough client interview process—we refer to it as C.P.S. (Case Preparation Services). This review entails a complete documentation of their assets, liabilities, annuities, living expenses, mortgages, special needs, bequests, goals, travel plans, housing changes, etc. In other words, a friendly conversation. This will exude confidence and a willingness to open themselves up to your suggestions.

Today's Seniors should not be viewed as a "one size fits all" community. This is a diverse group of people with different needs and thought processes. They still have dreams and desires. This part of their life didn't end when they hit the sixty-five-year mark. Many are "life long learners" and are opened to different ideas. They all, for the most part, crave and desire two things—RESPECT and RESPONSIVE SERVICE.

TRILOGY is not a new concept. It's the type of sales approach I was raised on. This "consultative or counseling approach" is a product of Tom Wolfe, with "Capital Needs Analysis," Joe Gandolfo, "Selling is 98% Understanding Human Nature and 2% Product Knowledge," Ben Woodson, "The Set of the Sail," Ben Feldman (maybe the greatest), Sydney Friedman, Jack Peckinpaugh, John Savage and many other great ones. I was fortunate to have known many of the above and heard all of them. I believe that Trilogy and C.P.S. are the concepts that will separate the have and have-not agents in this decade.

Chapter 30

Safety Standards

We have seen all of the independent testing of vehicles, car seats, medicine, breast implants, foods, and other lifestyle items. These reports tell us which cars are safer in a head-on collision. The government also advises us as to which foods can cause hardening of the arteries and potentially shortening our lives. The studies also let us know which cribs are better for our babies or the side effects that can accompany the prescription your physician ordered. I could go on and on, but the point is that these reports are based on *safety*.

Sure, we see the "performance" commercials on cars, the extra distance with a particular golf ball, or the extra "zip" you will get from some new medicine or vitamin enhancement. But please don't lose sight of the main ingredient of most surveys. It's *safety*. Is that what most Americans are concerned about? I think so. It only makes sense to take a tip from the experts. Let's examine.

If safety is the number one concern, why do we have to promise rates of return that may or may not be achieved? SAFETY FIRST! That's the motto!! Isn't that what we do? We provide safety in every product we offer. That's why our business is so great. Our clients don't expect something for nothing. They want safety and security. They want to stay in the world in which they have become accustomed, while safely knowing they can handle their current and future financial needs. Our clients don't want to be a burden to anyone. So my tip for the day—for every day, really—is PLAY IT SAFE!! That's what our clients want, that's what we have to offer and that's what we should sell!

Chapter 31

"Survey Says…"

Surveys and polls are conducted everyday for numerous products and services. We tend to accept this information as gospel. I am always a little leery of the findings. Many factors can affect the results. For example, who's asking the questions and compiling the information? Do they have a prejudiced view towards the subject matter? Also, how did they get the information? Were the people interviewed giving their real and true thoughts, or were they telling the interviewers what they thought they were supposed to say?

The financial services industry is no different. Survey results are telling us the "keys to success" in various markets as a result of various studies. I don't think we are getting the straight scoop. I surely wouldn't bet the ranch on their findings. So, what are we supposed to do?

A good example and illustration is the Senior Market. Everyone has "the answer"—"Our seminar system will earn you double last years income!" Or, "Our script is exactly what the senior wants to hear!" Or, "These are their greatest concerns!" How did they get this information? Also, I've noticed that the approach is basically the same as it was pre-9/11 and pre-stock market meltdown.

I've been doing my own surveys lately. Where? It might surprise you—the grocery store! I watch to see if most seniors buy brand name products or generic/house brands. Do they buy *Tropicana*™ or Kroger™ orange juice? Are they over-buying? Are they utilizing the "earlybird specials" at restaurants? Do most of them purchase $ 20 *Merlots* or the $ 9 big bottle? I do the same thing in the drugstore. (You should too!) Go right to the pharmacy and listen. That's a survey. These people are concerned. They remember World War II and they remember depressions and recessions. They want to hang on to as much of their money as possible for as long as possible. They are not scared, but they are concerned.

Talk to your clients and prospects about what's important to them. Let them talk first. Listen. Discuss their fears and needs. The information that you gather will allow not only for the chances of a sale, but also for the development of a great client. An agent recently told me that responses to seminars and results were declining. I asked, "What are you sending out to get them to the seminar and what are you saying in the seminar?"

His response, "The same thing that I've been doing for the last three years."

I assured him that he can expect the same results going forward. The world has changed. Are you changing with it? "Survey says…you'd better!"

Chapter 32

A Balancing Act

Americans in either a "pre-"or "current-retirement" stage have many financial factors to consider. The rules of the game have changed. The elder "youngsters," people between the ages of 55 and 70, have to re-examine their financial situation, including, though not limited to, their insurance portfolios. They must make the decision at some point to play it safe. They will take some money off the table—their "at-risk" money. The shortened time makes it imperative that they transfer a percentage of their nest egg to a safe money place. Hurricanes, high oil prices, potential housing bubbles, Chapter 11s, the "War on Terror," and other events play havoc with people's at risk money. People want to quit worrying and play it safe. That's where we come in. Consider the following:

- Social Security was never intended to take care of all or even most of our retirement needs. The tax for social security was approximately $50 per year from 1935 to 1955. Why? Because people only received benefits for six months (if they, in fact, lived to 65).
- More than 60,000 people will live past 100 next year.

So, let's not forget payout annuities—SPIAs. Congress sure isn't! We will see reduced taxation for Americans who move 401(k) money to SPIAs upon retirement. Let's make sure we are ready to assist!

Nursing home health care needs will increase. The female spouse is at risk. WHY? More women go into nursing homes or need home health care. WHY?

- Women live longer;
- Men can't take care of women;
- Women will do everything they can to keep the man at home.

Make sure your clients have either long term care coverage, annuities with nursing home liquidity features, life policies that allow you to utilize the death benefits as nursing home or home health care benefits, and/or Medicaid planning.

We also need to review our clients' insurance portfolios. Do they have adequate life insurance? Probably not. Use a portion of the penalty-free withdrawal in the annuity to fund a life policy thereby providing a tax free benefit. Or, how about annuitizing the SPIA over five to ten years to fund the policy and spread out the taxable gain.

Also, you should remind your clients that the majority of their lifetime medical expenses will occur in the last six months of their lives. They need to re-examine everything, and you are the person to do it.

Here's are two great opening questions to ask your prospects:

"How long did it take you to accumulate your nest egg? How long do you think it will last in a nursing home?"

As you begin to explain how you can help balance safety and liquidity while protecting them from catastrophic emergencies, you will win their confidence, and they will understand that this is no "act"— it's the real deal!

Chapter 33

Preserve, Protect, and Defend…

These three words are heard every four years at the inauguration of the President of the United States. These words rang even truer at the "Fourth of July" celebration, 2002. The events of September 11th reinforced America's pride in their country and their belief in its system of government. Unfortunately, it took this tragic loss of life to see "Old Glory" flying once again on so many of America's front porches. It reminded us that this is a country and way of life worth preserving, protecting, and defending!

We called our brave soldiers, and those of our allies, into action in Iraq. We once again experienced the loss of life that accompanies such a campaign. Because we are a society based on independence and freedom for all, so many have given the ultimate sacrifice throughout our history.

It's easy to lose focus. We are all extremely busy with our everyday lives. We are consumed with so many responsibilities that we often forget those who are defending our freedoms around the world. Now, I'm not suggesting that we dwell on the past tragedy in New York nor the war on terror. I'm just suggesting that we can never forget that we are responsible for our country's safekeeping.

I'm not suggesting, either, that we all are supposed to bear arms and join a militia. I do believe, however, that we are defending our way of life when we defend and honor—free speech, freedom of religion, racial tolerance, the importance of family, and the entrepreneurial flavor that made our country what it was, what it is, and what it will be tomorrow.

Defending our way of life also has financial connotations. How many times have we used, or heard the phrase, "we want to keep you in the world you have become accustomed to"? This is a timeless message, one that is truer today than ever.

There are two distinct yet important groups that benefit from single premium products. Yes, I said—plural—"products." These groups are annuities (both deferred and immediate) and single premium life (both universal life and whole life). These groups are for the retirees (65+) and the baby boomers. Let's quickly examine both.

THE RETIREES

We are all well aware of the magnitude of this market. Our annuity products provide retirees with either tax deferred build-up or an income stream that they cannot outlive (plus many other benefits in both products). The single premium life product is perfect for the senior who has money for which he/she has no immediate need. This is the "retirement inheritance money" we have been hearing about. Is this block of money suited for a single premium life product with a TAX FREE death benefit? Can a senior obtain quality life plans at an advanced age? Does it make sense? YOU·BE THE JUDGE.

Now, what about the second market group?

THE BABY BOOMERS

They are retiring everyday. They are in a perilous situation. They must soon change from accumulators to people receiving distributions. They must also make sure that they outpace inflation while staying "in their own world." Do our present SPIAs do that? Is this the time to "DO THE SPLITS" (split annuity)? A *Wall Street Journal* article says that 4 - 6% of the baby boom generation is retiring every year. Richard Reilly, former President and CEO of Allmerica Financial Corporation, said that by 2012, more than 13% of the population, controlling 80% of investable retirement assets in the U.S. will be retired. What a market! What an opportunity! And what a need for a "professional" planner!

FACTS:
- A healthy 65 year old will live to 87.5 or longer
- IRA rollovers will continue to increase by double digit percentages over the next 10—15 years
- Many people are living into their 90s.

QUESTION:

Is today's baby boomer factoring in a 95 to 100 year life expectancy when planning distribution? I don't know.

So, we have an opportunity to

1. PRESERVE their way of life in retirement. I believe an equity index annuity is part of the prescription.
2. PROTECT. Guarantee of principal is definitely there with our tax deferred products.
3. DEFEND against a reduction in lifestyle in their distribution phase. Helping them with quality SPIAs and other unique products that are on the drawing board.

Part III

Think About It

Chapter 34

Speed Bump

The art of driving an automobile has become second nature for Americans today. For most of us, our cars are among our most prized possessions. In addition to the "cool" factor, our cars represent something even more important—our freedom—our ticket to go wherever we want, whenever we want. Some of us enjoy driving just for the sake of driving even if we have no particular destination. This sort of random driving activity often proves to be the best way to find our new "favorite places." So, a warning to anyone who might try to take away or limit the use of the all American car from all Americans: don't!

Allow me to return to the idea of driving as a "second nature" activity. Think about it for a moment. You go into the garage (don't forget to open the door), put your keys in the ignition, back out, and go. You are not consciously thinking about using the accelerator on the right or the brake on the left. You don't have to think about slowing down for oncoming cars, stopping at each light, or turning on your signal when you want to turn. You just drive and assume a safe journey. Never a problem! Right? I don't think so. Please read on.

We drive and we see "Right Lane Closed—2 Miles Ahead." We either move over to the left or we are "cheaters" and fly down the right lane hoping some Good Samaritan will let us in at the end of the merging lane. They mostly do (even to the dismay of the other cussing drivers). We might see, "Construction Zone Ahead, Slow Down, Speed Limit 40 MPH!!" We may not test that sign too much because it also reads, "Let Them Work…Let Them Live—Fine $500." That gets our attention!

A school bus stops and puts out the stop sign; a dog runs across the road; you hit a squirrel; a bird flies into your windshield; a salt truck blows salt onto your shiny hood, and up ahead, a seat belt checkpoint comes into view. WHEW! These are but a few of the challenges we all face during the course of our "normal" driving routine. We don't get rattled; we just work within the system and continue our journey.

In my case, the worst impediment is the speed bump. Why? First, often I don't see a speed bump until it's too late, and when I hit it, it scares the *you-know-what* out of me! Second, I might see the speed bump but not believe that it is as high as it really is. It's such an annoying "thump" and awful sound as my car and I become airborne for a moment. It must be the shock effect. It knocks me out of my comfort zone. I either complain or kick myself for not paying attention. I then drive on without thinking of or anticipating the next bump.

Now, isn't that how we respond to challenges in life sometimes? The unexpected speed bumps rock us, yet we forget about each event and fail to prepare ourselves mentally for the next one. We're not perfect. We want to be optimistic and not dwell on future problems. That is the way we are supposed to respond.

Consider the "lowly" but so important speed bumps in life: what they are—*just small obstacles to slow us down*); what they are NOT designed to do to us—*they should NOT wreck our cars and throw us into a ditch*), and, finally, what they are supposed to do—*be a warning and a reminder that there may be more obstacles ahead.*

Speed bumps in life are annoying sometimes, but they are important for a variety of reasons. They get our attention and let us know that we need to stay on our toes, watch out, and concentrate on the task at hand. They are not supposed to cripple us, make us live in fear, or totally derail us from our paths.

So, put your keys in the ignition, back out, put the car in gear, and proceed. There will be many more speed bumps in our lives. Recognize them for what they are and you will successfully arrive at your destination.

Hey! I gotta drive! I'm late for an appointment!

Chapter 35

Every Day Is Mother's Day

One of the morning's news shows reported an interesting statistic. A research company, www.salaries.com, came up with the salary that a "stay at home" mom with two children would be earning in the "paying" workforce. That number is $135,000! That's the replacement cost based on hours worked and services provided. The number of hours worked by a mother with an outside job was over one hundred. The overtime pay alone would cripple an employer! Startling numbers— these numbers may surprise you, but not most moms.

The news program really got me thinking during my morning drive to work. I reflected on all the things my mom did for my siblings, my dad, and me. She was the "plant manager." Things didn't function well unless mom did it. I'm confident that most of you experienced the same situation while you were growing up. It was somewhat easier for moms in the 50s, 60s, and 70s. Most moms did not work outside the home. There was no stigma attached to being a "stay at home" mom. But times have changed. Many women work outside the home and still handle the vast majority of the "motherly" duties. Tough job! Much of this choice was personal, while some work for economic reasons. Both types of moms work their "you know what's" off. But, do we let the moms know this? Do they really know how we feel about them and the respect that we have for what they do? In my case, not often enough!

My wife, Ann, was a teacher. She quit teaching when our oldest child, Nick, was born. She chose to devote her life to raising the kids. Please don't think that she dropped out of all other projects. She was president of every PTO, the full time volunteer, the free consultant for the school system, full time driver, homework supervisor, great partner, and, fortunately for me, the best cook in town! She started doing some event planning as the kids got older and now assists me in our business.

The problem is that her products, the kids, are now "out of the factory" and in the market. She raised them properly and they are all doing well but they don't need her full attention every day. Unfortunately, this stage in life comes very abruptly. There isn't time to prepare. Moms may even wonder if it was worth leaving the workforce. Don't get me wrong, you don't have to stay at home to be a good mom. I do know that I, many times, don't give my wife enough thanks for making this her choice. She doesn't look at this choice as a sacrifice, but only as what she felt she should do.

So, I wanted and need to tell Ann what I'm telling you (hint, if you haven't done so already, you might follow my lead!). My wife is the greatest mom in the world. I am the luckiest man to have a woman that would support the children and me before she considered herself. Unconditional love and caring for others—isn't that what a mom is all about? So, on Mother's Day, before I go babbling about everything I've done the week before, I am going to wish her a Happy Mother's Day! I want her to know that I appreciate everything she has done and still continues to do.

So, let's all tell our moms that what they did and what they do is important. For us married guys, count your lucky stars and let your wife know the same. The world wouldn't work well without moms—if men had to give birth, we would have a population shortage.

Chapter 36

More Income Or Higher Commissions?

This is a tough question for many sales people to answer. It seems especially problematic for people in the financial services industry. You see, many falsely believe that they are one in the same. They think, and wrongly in my opinion, that one cannot have more income without higher commissions. I believe just the opposite. I believe that excessively high commissions can lead to lower income. Okay, before you think I've completely lost my mind, allow me to explain…because I do want high commissions…fair commissions. But, neither at my expense nor my client's expense. Let's investigate.

The pricing of products in the financial services industry is not, as many companies would have you believe, a great big mystery. Let's first look at the fixed annuity. The two biggest components of an annuity are 1) expenses, and 2) investment returns. You sell an annuity, send it to the insurance company, they invest the money, issue a policy and pay you a commission. Each year they take the gross investment return, subtract the expense and there's the profit (your commissions are part of the expense). This is a thumbnail sketch of product design. No insults are intended for the fine home office professionals that work behind the scene. So, let's dig a little deeper.

Commissions that are higher than the norm need to come from somewhere. Think the insurance company is settling for a lower profit? Think again. So, renewal rates will suffer, service may decline and no one is happy long term. Gives you a *quick fix* but nothing to help your practice survive and thrive.

Scenario #2—Agent *beats up* on the IMO (Insurance Marketing Organization) for higher commissions. IMO makes less money and gives less in return. It's only human nature and anyone that tells you different is in a different world and may not survive very long anywhere! So, what's the answer? A happy medium!

- Products that are good for the consumer—a fair return
- Products that are good for the life insurance company. Fair profits that allow for top notch services and fair compensation.'
- Products priced fairly for the agent. Commission rates that pay you for the professional role you serve.
- Products with fair compensation for the IMO. Enough profit to help the producers develop marketing plans, business plans and sales packages. A system that allows the producer open access to an organization that will assist the producer in his/her quest for success.

In summary, we need a fair playing field for all. Systems that tilt too far, either way, can be disastrous for all parties. So, I believe that the numbers speak for themselves. Too high a commission can mean fewer sales. Why? No help from the companies and dissatisfied consumers. Fair commissions with support from IMOs and companies coupled with a quality product will lead to more sales which mean more income. Think about it. It only makes sense.

Chapter 37

The State of Our Business

The financial services industry has gone through some unbelievable changes over the last twenty-five years. Maybe "unbelievable" is the wrong word to use. Maybe the proper phrase would be "short sighted." The industry definitely has had a strategy. Its strategy has been to increase profitability while systematically reducing the resources available to field management in regards to recruiting, managing, training, and motivating its organizations.

First, the industry pitted career managers and general agents against the producing agents by increasing the producer compensation while reducing the compensation formulas of recruiting general agents. Part of the strategy was to lower overall compensation, delivering lower cost products and taking advantage of unique plans (such as universal life), reap record premium dollars, and invest in double digit bond rates, real estate. and for some, private placements. The strategy may have made sense at the time, but it failed miserably. Look at the facts.

Insurers projected 10% to 11% or 12% returns on universal life. Rates started decreasing and they started to chase yields. Some went into real estate. The bottom dropped out of the market and many companies faced significant financial challenges. What would they do now? Further reduce services to the field? But then, it went all the way to the producers in the field.

Enter the Insurance Marketing Organizations (IMOs) to whom some refer as "wholesalers." The insurance industry basically began to forsake the career agencies. They gave the gross compensation to the IMO. The IMO recruited representatives (experienced agents only), and provided products, training, and back office services. Again, sound strategy. However, there was a problem—they had no new recruits. IMOs are not paid to recruit new agents, sell the profession, nor train and assist in the growth of the neophyte producer. So, we all began to recycle each other's contracted producers.

IMOs started to reduce services as they were squeezed by reduced margins. Agents were cutting their best deals. They were milking as much as they could from the IMOs. Who could blame them? Agents were now working the senior market and it was huge! Plenty of companies were offering annuities and senior market products. The good producers could hold out for the best deals, write a large amount of business, and then bid themselves out to other IMOs. But hold on! Another storm was circling the business—low interest rates—meaning lower yields on insurers' assets. But they kept selling. They believed that rates would surely go up. Again they took *safe* bets—bets like *ENRON*, *TYCO*, *WORLDCOM* and others. Well, at the time, it *seemed* like a good strategy. These were all safe companies offering good rates on their bonds. Who would have thought that these bonds, in a relatively short time, would go for pennies on the dollar or less?

But tomorrow will be better, right? The insurance companies kept writing business. They were utilizing all their capital and surplus. They weren't able to raise equity and couldn't afford new debt service. Some went out of business. Some stopped selling and reduced crediting rates to the guarantees. The large companies ruled the insurance airways and began to set the rules. The competition began to shrink. Commissions were slashed, products all began to look alike, and the agents began to see these products began as commodities. But, the industry had another strategy up their sleeves—financial institutions and "buy direct." If they could just eliminate the agent's commissions, all would be *fine*; however, they had forgotten one thing—***INSURANCE IS SOLD NOT BOUGHT***!!

This is a *Reader's Digest* review of the last twenty-five years. We still have many chapters to write. There can be a happy ending for everyone, but, everyone is going to have to be realistic! We all need help. That's right, help.

Everyone brags about "service." What is good service? I don't see it with most companies. Those of us in the field should not expect better service. Better service will be less than we experienced years ago. So, how about help? How about helping the agent maintain a great profession? How about help in business planning? How about help in case preparation? How about an IMO that acts as an agency manager?

In summary, IMOs that "help" the individual agent, financial planner, or consultant successfully will win the day. Let's forget a better mousetrap. Let's let our guards down and look for help. After thirty years as a successful MDRT agent, career agency builder, marketing company owner, and president of one of America's fastest growing annuity companies, I have decided to have The Ohlson Group focus and specialize in one main area. That area is <u>help</u>.

What does that mean? How about assisting you in every aspect of your business career today, tomorrow, and into the future? The concept is hard to define and I'm sure I'll have my critics; however, I'm convinced that I know how to help, that I have been helpful, and that I'm committing our organization to giving you the same benefits I was fortunate to have in my career.

HELP is good at all ages, regardless of experience. The busier you are, the more help you need. Let me rephrase that—***the more help you deserve***!

Let's help each other. This may be the "strategy" that our industry needs. I'm looking forward to making it happen.

Chapter 38

Supply Chain Delivery System

The expression, "Supply Chain Delivery System," has been around for quite awhile. It refers to the entire process of getting a finished product to the end user—the consumer. Often, the economy dictates the extent to which CEO's and senior management pay attention to this process. As a matter of fact, many CEO's consider this process an enormous hassle. The reason may be that implementing such a process is a *"roll-up-your-sleeves, plan it out, and do it right"* process! Nonetheless, this process is extremely important today. It's important in both a good economy and a bad economy.

Consider the financial advisor's role. You have an appointment with a prospect. You present your credentials describing your experience and knowledge. You then interview your client regarding his/her current financial situation, current needs, future and current concerns, and financial goals. You set another appointment to make a presentation. At that meeting, you motivate your client to act, and you consummate a financial transaction (sale). Now you can relax, right? NO WAY!! You've just started the *SUPPLY CHAIN DELIVERY SYSTEM*. You are a long way from done. Keep your fingers crossed and hope that all participants in this system are as motivated regarding this sale as you. Let's peek behind the curtains and see what's going on "backstage."

Let's assume that the sale was a fixed deferred annuity (a life sale would have additional components, such as a medical exam, APS, MIB, phone interview, etc.). Here are the steps in the process:

- You send the application, check or 1035 or transfer form, possible replacement forms and any other suitability or compliance form required by your state (you or your staff, hopefully, made copies) either to the insurance company or your IMO (Insurance Marketing Organization).
- *The recipient opens the file, logs the information, assigns a policy number, sends required forms to current financial institution (if replacement involved), and begins the policy issue stage. If it's a cash*

deal, here's what happens:
- The policy is printed
- *Commission payment requested*
- Information posted online
- *Options purchased, if EIA*
- Policy and commission check are packaged
- *Policy sent to you*
- Commission check sent or automatically deposited

OR,

- *Call back dates inserted in a 1035 or transfer situation*
- A staff person stays on top of activities
- *You are able to retrieve information online*
- The insurance company assists you in finalizing this transaction
- *You receive policy*
- Deliver to your client
- *You receive referrals*
- You send thank you letter
- *Client receives thank you letter upon receipt of delivery forms from the insurance company*
- You continue to build your business and all parties are satisfied.

WHEW! That's a lot of work, but all of your sales turn out this way, right? Not if you're dealing in today's financial services arena. Productivity—increased production—is what carriers are demanding. Not all of them are concerned about the successful culmination and completion of a finely tuned supply chain delivery system. It's too expensive, too time consuming, and too boring. Top line and bottom line numbers are what get people promoted, not the nitty-gritty. So what's an advisor to do?

First, you should associate with a top quality IMO that will help shepherd your business through the home offices. This association can prove to be more valuable than any of the "get rich quick schemes" that you have probably read about. Second, you must take ownership of this process. <u>You</u> are driving the bus. Don't leave anything to chance. Finally, work as a team with your IMO. More and more companies are requiring the IMOs to do the jobs that the insurance companies performed in the past. Check out the experience and credentials of the

IMO you are dealing with. Many firms can offer products and compensation. The IMOs that believe that every step in this process is important are the IMOs that will allow you to maximize the usage of your *three most valuable assets*—TIME, MONEY, and MANPOWER!

It's been a long time coming, but effective delivery of products will be the biggest factor differentiating IMOs. These organizations will now have to put up or shut up. Financial advisors deserve, and should demand, top notch supply chain delivery systems! Remember, "NOTHING HAPPENS UNTIL SOMEBODY SELLS SOMETHING!" It's your effort, your client, and your compensation. Demand the best! If you are not getting it, do what your prospect would do—shop around.

Chapter 39

The Career Agency System

These words—the career agency system—seem very professional and timely to me. The word "career" means something more to me than just a "job," more than just earning a living. "Career" strikes me as something "very professional," something with substance.

The word "system" sounds as if a definite plan exists that is designed to give the agent (producer, advisor, planner, etc.) every possible chance for success. So why, if it seems to make so much sense, did our life insurance industry abandon this concept? There are many reasons the industry uses as a rationale for leaving the agents behind. This, however, is not the time or place for that discussion. Yet, there are still a handful of companies that embrace the career system. The embrace or hug they give the agents is not as warm as it used to be, but it's still the only hug that most agents will ever receive.

I had the great fortune of building, from scratch, one of American General's successful career agencies in the late 1970s and early 1980s. I take great pride in the number of agents that I hired and trained who are extremely successful in the financial service industry. Many of them, in fact, are more financially successful than I will ever become. You see many of their pictures and names in the various trade magazines. These people learned the basic prospecting, presentations, and closing techniques. They learned how they should and could build and maintain a lifelong profession. No one had to "require" continual education. Everyone understood, in those days, that all "career" agents would study through the various professional organizations: the LUTC (Life Underwriting Training Council) and/or the CLU (Chartered Life Underwriter), or ChFC (Chartered Financial Consultant) or the CFP (Certified Financial Planner) designation.

A number of my "green pea" agents went on to finish MBAs or JD degrees. Some are fee-based RIAs (Registered Investment Advisors). The Million Dollar Round Table (MDRT) was the starting point for claiming success in this great industry. Sounds like it was working well.

So, what happened? Why the change?

The advent of universal life and the insurance company's "chase for the investment yields" were just the beginning of the changes. Companies didn't believe that the cost of training, marketing, and sales assistance was worth the investment. So, they closed the system down, cut the managers' or general agents' compensation, and raised commissions to the new independent agent. They also counted on the new product's ability to raid other companies' products. In other words, the biggest "replacement war" our business has ever seen began—and it continues in some form today.

One big problem the companies didn't consider—the agents began cannibalizing their own businesses. Agents stopped getting the referrals and lived off the replacements. And, they built new lifestyles based on this compensation. They bought bigger homes and fancier cars, and they stopped investing in themselves. Then the bottom fell out—there were no more policies to replace, UL illustrations and projections, didn't materialize, the agent didn't know how to "re-start" their businesses, and many of them left this great profession. The result of this upheaval, according to LIMRA (Life Insurance Management & Research Association), is that the average age of today's agent is fifty-five years. The sorry state of our industry, however, is great news for you.

The current retiree market is huge. It will only get bigger with the aging of the boomers. You'll find many needs to handle and new clients to help you "re-build" our system. Yes, there are tremendous opportunities ahead if you are ready for and aware of them.

There is, however, one missing link. Where is the "CAREER"? Where's the "AGENCY"? Where's the "SYSTEM"? The answers rest with today's Insurance Marketing Organization (IMOs), not with Brokerage Agencies, nor with the Wholesalers. They push products on a spreadsheet and live and die with the hottest products and highest commissions. But what do you do when, "What you've got is not hot?" The answer is in assisting the agent in his/her career development and in providing marketing assistance, research capabilities, and an educational forum.

Service is a given. Agents are demanding more. And, they deserve it. So what is our industry, and our agents, to do? We all need a "sit-down." The sit-down can be on the phone—producer to IMO. Each party states what he/she can bring to the table. Each party needs to know, "What's in it for me?" Relationships must be strengthened or developed. IMOs need to do more than offer products. They need to be your "observation deck." They need to let you know what's coming down the road. What legislative changes will affect their lives? What will Medicare and Medicaid reform do to the planner's business? How will new suitability rules affect the "fixed life and annuity business?"

So far, I've given just a snapshot of what's facing us. I'm sitting on the deck of my beach house in South Carolina. As I look out at the crashing waves, I'm reminded that the tides <u>do</u> change. Some tidal changes affect us negatively and some positively. We do know one thing. There will always be tidal changes. A big tidal change is currently affecting our business. The waves will be bigger and the crashes more intense. The sailors who survive and thrive during these tropical disturbances will be aboard vessels that experienced and professional captains are piloting. Through the assistance of modern technology, they will see many storms before they "arrive." They will also rely on their years of experience and their "gut feelings" when they sound the alarm.

The sky is now a pristine blue. There is barely a cloud to disturb this peaceful moment. The tide is receding and I feel that all is well. It is. Our greatest days lie ahead. Those who choose a wise captain will have more security and success. It's time to choose a team…and a plan. Is this the start of the "new and improved, slightly modified, yet still independent" career agency system? I think so. That's why I'm looking for additional sea-worthy crew members.

I'm now going to take a beach walk and get my thoughts together. I'll be back in the office in a couple of days. Recruiting season is now upon us and I'm looking for some professionals who understand and want to buy into my concept. Give me a call or write me a note. Let me know what you are looking for. I think I can help you find it.

Chapter 40

"You've Got A Friend"

I had a wonderful evening last night. It was my wife's birthday and we took the kids to a James Taylor concert. The evening was perfect. Temperature was about 65 degrees with virtually no humidity. We were with our three adult kids—a great family outing. It's always great to get everyone together—I know you understand…there's simply nothing like family!

I've always liked James Taylor. I believe that he has become somewhat of an "institution." People will fondly look back at entertainers and I think the majority will agree that James Taylor had made and left his mark. He sings and writes his songs from experience. Many of his songs originated from bad times and many from good times. He always knows when to ignite the crowd with an active beat. People relate to James Taylor and view him as a friend.

Why does James Taylor have this "friend relationship" with his audiences? He treats them with the same dignity and respect that he seeks to obtain. He's not braggadocios. He doesn't make a flashy entrance. He gives the crowd what they paid to see and hear. He works hard (two encores the night we saw him), takes time to give autographs, and shake hands with his fans. Plus, at the end of his performance he says, simply but sincerely, "Thanks! Thanks for coming and see ya next time!"

We need friends in the financial services business. We are lucky if we can find an insurance company that truly views us as a friend. I truly viewed the agent as a friend during my ten-year tenure as president of a major life insurance company. It was a simple thing for me because I had spent twenty years in the field as agent, general agent, and wholesaler.

Sadly, I don't think it's that way with most insurance company executives today. If that's the case, then, as Taylor sings, "you've got a friend"…that is, a friend that's a marketing company/wholesaler. You need a firm that is sympathetic and empathetic towards your goals and desires. A firm that treats you as family. A firm that realizes that you are their most valuable asset.

Friendship is a two-way street. It brings about certain responsibilities and expectations. Friendships require work, consideration, and commitment. As you all know, you will get precisely from a friendship what you put into it. It is a relationship, whether personal or business.

So, pick a firm with which you are proud to associate. See if there is a chance for a mutually profitable and enjoyable relationship. Then go to work. Everyone keeps their side of the bargain—at least, that's the way it's supposed to work! I know that it can be lonely out there sometimes. I've been there. I have experienced those unfulfilled promises, the personal setbacks, the tribulations and the great triumphs. I've walked a mile in both your shoes and in the home office shoes. So, I thank you, sincerely, for all your friendships! I hope to develop more relationships with America's finest—the financial services advisors!

Chapter 42

Home Movies

My wife and I spent part of a rainy Saturday looking at some old home movies. What memories! When did my hair start turning gray? The years pass by so quickly. Watching these old films brought back fond memories, and triggered some painful emotions as well. I was happy watching our three wonderful children growing up again before my eyes. At the same time, I experienced a little sadness knowing that we can never duplicate those days. Understand that I don't believe our best years are behind us. It's just that I recognized that that was a period in our lives that only happens once. It was a time to treasure and be glad about. But, I'm not one of those who longs for "the good old days". There are plenty of "Good New Days" ahead of us.

One of the home movies showed my wife, Ann, helping our then one-year-old son, Joe, learn how to walk. (Joe is now 22 years old!) He would make those first, hesitant steps, start to fall, and regain his balance. Ann would sometimes have to save him from hitting the deck. The other fact I witnessed in this film that moved me was that Ann was very pregnant and gave birth to our daughter Kiley a couple weeks later. But, we were in the front yard for another reason. It was our oldest child's first day of school and I wanted to be there to film him walking home. Many of you know this son—Nick, our marketing director at The Ohlson Group.

In the film, Nick was walking with his best friend, Andy. I asked, "What did you do in school today?" They replied that they learned a new song. They proceeded to sing it to us. I'm glad I was there during that mid-afternoon in August to experience this time and to get it on tape.

There is a moral to this story. While watching the film, I was reminded how lucky I was to be in the insurance business. I was self-employed and able to be home without asking permission—without having to give some phony reason as to why I needed to leave work. The insurance business gave and continues to give me the opportunity to experience things that many other people miss. It allowed me the opportunity to coach virtually every sport, to be head of the booster club, to attend piano recitals, and to be involved in my children's lives. Our business has been good for Ann, too. She has served as parent teacher organization president in each school our children attended. It was a tremendous time in our lives!

We are very lucky. We are in the greatest business in the world! The more good we do for our customers, the more money we make. Plan your work and work your plan! When you do, you'll have plenty of time to participate in the most important component of your life— YOUR FAMILY! Don't miss a minute of it!

So, dust off the camera and start shooting. And remember, there are a lot more memories ahead. They will be different, but they will still be great!

Chapter 42

In Memory Of...

Memorial Day provides a perfect platform for us to take a moment and put our lives in perspective. We have the opportunity to reflect on the sacrifices made by millions of Americans to preserve and protect our freedom—freedoms that most of the world will never experience:

- freedom to say what we think,
- freedom to worship whenever we desire,
- freedom to choose our electorate.

These freedoms, that we often take for granted, make us the envy of the world. I say this in spite of an American and worldwide press that would have us believe that we are despised and detested. In fact, we are what others only dream about.

I had the opportunity of having the responsibility for growing a Luxembourg and Bermuda insurance company. We purchased that company in December of 1993. It was a small ($ 79 million in assets) company without product and without representatives. I volunteered to take responsibility and headed off to Europe to build a field force, oversee the operations, and turn the company into a profitable organization. We were, by far, the smallest of our competitors, plus I had never been to Europe!

My staff of twenty spoke nineteen languages! I felt a little insecure knowing only bare bones Italian that I had learned from my mother and grandparents, a little French, and a ton of grammatical errors!

But, I had one great advantage over my staff—I was an American. That didn't grant me immediate acceptance, but it gave me a basis from which to help grow that little company into a force to be reckoned with. I assured my staff that I didn't want to change their culture or heritage. I wanted to combine the best of American ingenuity and entrepreneurialism with the traditions, pride, and culture of Europe. We were off to the races! A true success story.

The Europeans hungered for American marketing. They liked the fact we made decisions quickly. They also liked the fact that everyone, including myself, would get their "hands dirty." There was no job too menial for the head guy!

I was proud of America and never hid that fact. My new and ongoing European friends took me on many tours. In Sweden, I went to the border and saw the Russian tanks standing guard. I took the train from Milan to Switzerland and saw the remnants of Nazi occupation. I saw the US Cemetery in Luxembourg which looks like Arlington in Virginia. The head stones are shiny and the gates are rimmed in gold. American flags fly in abundance. The locals care for this cemetery. General George Patton's birthday is a national holiday! Contrast this with the German cemetery 50 yards away that is overgrown, dark, and dingy.

Oh, some Europeans and others will disagree. Some governments go to great lengths to distance themselves. But, they admire and respect what we have been able to do in just over two hundred years. Maybe that's why we are referred to as "The Great Experiment".

So, our forefathers have given us an opportunity to chart our own course and seek out our own destiny. This opportunity was, and still is, protected by Americans who gave and continue to give their lives so that we can continue our wonderful way of life.

I can never give to America what our brave men and women have given—their lives. I can only thank them. I can also put my "woes" in perspective, live my life, work my job, and be the best I can be. It would be an insult to our soldiers to do less.

Chapter 43

A Moving Experience

The weekend of June 5–6, 2004 will be permanently etched in my mind. The sixtieth anniversary of the Invasion of Normandy made me extremely proud to be an American. I have always been proud of my American citizenship. But, the supreme sacrifices made by men and women sixty years earlier brought a lump in my throat and a tear to my eye. It makes most of the things I gripe about today seem so trivial in comparison.

The weekend also brought about sadness with the passing of our former President, Ronald W. Reagan. I knew that this day would come as he had been in decline for the past ten years. Still, it was an enormous loss for America and for me. "The Great Communicator" brought pride back to America. He was able to enlist the hearts and souls of Americans, and that enabled him to bring about sweeping reforms and changes in which he believed so dearly. His two landslide election victories show how America, and much of the world, felt about him.

On that late spring weekend, there was something else that struck me about this remarkable man. He had accomplished so much though he had come from so little. He made me take stock in what I have accomplished. It also made me "give myself a kick in the ass" to go out and do more. There is always time and we do live in the best country in the world.

Here are just a few of the things President Reagan accomplished:

- Grew up poor.
- Graduated from high school and was on the football, swim, and track teams.
- Was in the drama club and was president of his class.
- Was president of his class at Eureka College.
- Enlisted in the Army Reserve.
- Appeared in fifty movies.
- Was president of the Screen Actors Guild.

- Was a two-term governor of California.
- Was a two-term president of the United States of America.
- Brought about a new prosperity to America.
- Responsible for the fall of the Soviet Union and the Berlin Wall.
- Most popular president in modern history according to polls.

What does this have to do with our business? PLENTY! There is always a little more gas in our tanks! There's always another mountain to climb. There is always more that we can do with and for our families and clients. And we can strive to do it with the class, humor, integrity, and professionalism that President Reagan demonstrated throughout his remarkable and long life.

Thanks for allowing me to write this. I feel that I must now take advantage of all the great opportunities that America provides. I must also continually strive to do better. To do less would be an insult to those brave men on D-Day and to "Dutch"…President Ronald W. Reagan. May God bless his soul, and may God bless America!

Chapter 44

A Volunteer Army

I've just finished reading a wonderful book about Alexander the Great and his military strategies. This historic ruler has influenced many military organizations throughout the centuries. In recent history, our generals and fighting forces used much of Alexander's strategies during the first Gulf War. As I read of his exploits, I couldn't help but marvel at the way he ruled the countries he conquered with a variety of different governmental forms. Some were democratic, some were monarchies, and many were even dictatorial. Alexander had the keen sense to allow his vanquished foes to exist in the world to which they had become accustomed. He didn't feel that it was "my way or the highway."

I was also intrigued by the success his troops enjoyed in war even when the fiercest country in the world—Persia—vastly outnumbered them. What was Alexander's secret for success? There are far too many to mention here, certainly, but one of the most important keys to his success is that he believed firmly in an *all volunteer army*. The Greeks, the Persians, and other governments of the period forced military service upon their citizens. The Greeks required it for life! Alexander, on the other hand, believed that the best army was one into which individuals volunteered their service from a sense of duty, honor, patriotism, other values. It made sense to Alexander then; it makes sense today. I believe that is why the US Armed Forces are so strong today.

Among the many other attributes of Alexander's greatness, his education was certainly high on the list. Alexander's father, Philip, employed none other than Aristotle as a tutor. Philip wanted his son to understand people, understand human nature, and learn to anticipate people's needs. He was taught to be a good leader; consequently, his troops were eager to volunteer, were loyal followers, were ambitious, and became highly trained. Moreover, his men were both sympathetic and empathetic towards the needs of their vanquished foes. They understood that Alexander would do everything possible to keep them from harm's way. The troops also knew that Alexander would not ask them to do anything that he wouldn't do himself. They knew that Alexander was battle-tested, and he proved it time and time again by leading them into battle rather than observing from a safe distance behind the front lines.

We have adopted much of this same philosophy at The Ohlson Group. Of course, I'm not comparing myself to Alexander the Great, but after reading his biography, I do find similarities in the way we operate! We are:

- Highly trained;
- Sympathetic and empathetic regarding your goals and aspirations;
- Cognizant of the differences that abound in difficult parts of the country;
- Battle-tested (we were successful producers);
- Leaders in our industry (Life Members of MDRT, president of US and international companies);
- Experienced;
- Work with a volunteer "Producer Army" (we will release you at anytime and provide you with an "Honorable Discharge" to another IMO).

We are entering a new era in the financial services business. The insurance companies are transferring all service, marketing, and administrative duties to the IMOs (Insurance Marketing Organizations). Most do not want any soldiers (independent advisors) calling their headquarters. Hence, your lifeline to service and support is with the IMO. So, I'm looking for additional volunteers. No, I don't want an army like the Persians. Alexander and his Macedonians conquered the world with an army 10% the size of the Persians. Maybe we are like the modern day US Marines. We are looking for a "few good men and women." If you're interested, let's review your "battle plans." Let us assist you with new ideas, and let's march into battle together!

Everyone in our business will be joining an "army" soon. I hope you will join us. When you do, I think you will understand why we say, The Ohlson Group is "…a different experience."

Chapter 45

Window Washing

At our home, we have our windows washed professionally every fall and spring. We do wash them ourselves in between these two events, but we hire the professionals at least twice a year. We have a father and son team that can climb up three stories in the back of the house. They do a tremendous job. I'm fearful that I would be like Chevy Chase in the comedy "Christmas Vacation" if I attempted to scale that ladder. Again, these guys are pros.

It's always remarkable to look out during the spring and have such a clear view of the trees, yards, birds, and freshly planted spring flowers. It brings about a new perspective on life. The advent of spring, especially here in the Midwest, is exciting after the cold and snow we usually have to endure during our long Indiana winters.

We all need to do some personal window washing. We get so accustomed to seeing things one way—through life's "dirty windows"—that we assume it is the normal view. But, just like washing the windows in our homes, we can get a clearer view of what lies outside our haven of safety.

Here's a little window washing assignment for you.

Spend thirty minutes this week analyzing how you view your business. Take a piece of paper and apply the "Ben Franklin T" process. Put everything positive about your business on the left side and the negatives on the right side of the page. Now, ask yourself why you consider the right side items as negatives.

1. Do the negatives have some inherent opportunities?
2. Are you dodging the negatives, thereby cutting into the positives?
3. Can you eliminate or delegate to others the items you deemed negative?
4. Do some of the negatives become worse over time and could you eliminate the mental anguish by "nipping them in the bud?"

Many times we continue to operate, both personally and professionally, the way we have always operated in the past. We succumb to the "this is the way we've always done it" philosophy. But we should constantly be analyzing the way we are doing things. We should ask ourselves, "Am I missing some opportunities in the things I perceive as negatives?" Maybe there are some positives buried in there!

The only way we will find out if something positive is hidden among the negatives in our personal and business lives is to open our eyes and look. We need to get a clearer picture of <u>what</u> we are doing, <u>how</u> we are doing it, and <u>why</u> we are doing it. But, to accomplish this act of true perception, we must do as the song says, "I can see clearly now." And to see clearly, you might just need to do some professional window washing!

So, no matter what time of year it is right now, think of it as springtime. It's time for some serious window washing! So, roll up your sleeves, reserve some time for yourself, and start washing those windows of perception. You might just find the results to be magnificent! The view is the same, but the way you'll see after the task will be completely different!

Chapter 46

Corporate Memory

Early in my insurance career, I completed a two-week course titled 'Model-netics'. The course was the brainchild of Harold Hook, former Chairman & CEO of American General. The program is still in existence today under its corporate name 'Main Event Management'. Back in the 70s and 80s, the course was based on 151 business models. It was really a different business language that related to these models/diagrams. I still remember and use many of these models in my business and personal life. It might have been the best learning experience of my career. One of the models is of particular interest to me and, I hope, to you—corporate memory.

What is corporate memory? In simple terms, Corporate Memory is, "Not forgetting those who took you to the dance." In other words, don't forget the people who have assisted you and/or have been part of your early success. When the cash register is ringing, it's really easy to forget about the hard days. You should remember that those were hard days for those around you too. These loyal people bought into your dreams and vision. The ones who are still with you deserve your support, your thanks, and your respect. These people, among others, include your office assistants, fellow agents, and even vendors who may have extended credit to your organization.

Corporate Memory also plays into your personal life. What about your spouse? He or she was there when you were getting started. What about sacrifices they made early on in your business venture? Don't forget them!

In this day of instant gratification and our "what have you done for me lately" world, people have a tendency to forget "who took you to the dance". Trust me, we don't and won't at The Ohlson Group. We've been there too. There will always be the "new heroes" and "Monday morning quarterbacks" who will be the new stars. I like dancing with someone who knows my steps. Maybe we taught those steps to each other and we want to keep dancing.

I would like to personally thank each and every one of you for yesterday's business, today's business and tomorrow's business. So, don't put away those dancing shoes! As the song goes, "I hope you dance!"

Chapter 47

Tornado Warning

It's November and terrible tornadoes have touched down in Indiana, Ohio, and West Virginia and are moving towards the mid-Atlantic. Temperatures are at 70 degrees in Indianapolis on November 10th—what in the world is going on? Is it El Nino? Is it global warming? Or does it fall under the category of "s- -t happens?"

I believe that the weather, like life, brings about different cycles. Some are good; some are bad. The reaction to these events dictates how we will fare during the balance of our lives. The above-mentioned tornadoes brought about significant property damage, injuries, and unfortunate loss of life. The victims lives were snuffed out and the survivors had to deal with it.

We have had many examples of heroes since 9/11. They have always been there, but not as pronounced. The other heroes are the ones left behind. How can they deal with such tragedy? Planning your life is so important, but being prepared for your "personal tornado" is not usually considered.

We all have examples. One of my best friends is a physician. His youngest son died of cancer a little over a year ago. He was twenty-four years old and just finished medical school. Another good friend of mine has throat cancer. He will find out next week if he will need his tongue and voice box taken out (and, no, he has never smoked, is in perfect shape, principal of the largest high school in Indiana, and plays piano in his church choir). I have been able to watch these two individuals, and their families, deal with these unfortunate circumstances. I don't know if I could have been as strong as these people.

What's the point of this little diatribe? Well, I'm surely not trying to depress you. I am only suggesting that you kiss your spouse every day when you leave for work and every night before you close your eyes. You cannot hug your kids too much. Nothing is more important, including your job, than being at a child's or grandchild's special event.

Also, "blow it out sometimes"! I mean, HAVE FUN!! Stay out too late, dance too much, and party like you are in your 20s. Remember, we are leasing time; we don't own the next 10–20–30 years. Spread kindness, integrity, honesty, and pleasure among your family, friends. and clients. This will be your legacy. I am going to concentrate on these items as well. You never know when we might experience our own "personal tornado."

Chapter 48

Gray Hair and Receding Hairlines

I read an interesting article recently in one of our most respected trade magazines. The issue was dedicated to new agent recruiting, retention rates, and the demographics relating to people in the life insurance industry (the annuity sales person is part of this group). The information was startling. It summarized the opportunities and the challenges that are facing our great profession.

First off, the article focused on the handful of life companies that are still recruiting "new and inexperienced" agents. The number of companies in this arena continues to shrink. Here are some of the findings:

- Five-year retention rates hit an all time low. Only 11% are surviving.
- The average age of the field force today is 55 years old.
- There are not enough new agents joining the ranks to take the place of those dying or retiring.
- There will be a shortage of agents to take care of our insurance buying public.

What does this mean to America? Well, many Americans will die dangerously uninsured. There will be less money passed down to families to pay for education, mortgages, and charitable bequests. There will also be less cash value in the market. These cash value accounts have been used for emergencies and opportunities. Using the cash value in permanent life policies started many businesses. The potential economic impact to our country could be enormous!

What does all of this mean to us? Well, the opportunities for the professional, well-trained, knowledgeable, and honest financial services representative are tremendous!

- There will be less competition from other agents.
- Children of our clients will be our new clients, as neophyte agents won't call on them.

- Agencies will expand and hire new staff to handle the new servicing, marketing, and sales opportunities.
- The value of the professional's practices will increase.
- Life insurance companies will start to purchase agencies aggressively.
- Much, much more.

What about the competition?

Banks, Savings & Loans, Credit Unions, and broker-dealers will be our new competition. Branches will be set up in Wal-Mart, Target, and malls. People will start to seek out insurance since no one will be calling them. Time will fly by. Now is the time to re-examine your business plan. Make sure you are positioned to prosper in what may be ultimately referred to as "the golden years" of our business! Start thinking about adding new people with full heads of hair. The gray may be viewed as distinguished and knowledgeable, but fresh young legs will carry us on to the next decade.

Chapter 49

Guilt By Association

The financial services business finds itself under a microscope. We've all read about the mutual fund scandals, the illegal activities of CEO's and officers of some of America's largest companies, and the jail time that many of these people will now serve.

What about the insurance business? How is it doing? Let's focus on the life and annuity business. Pretty clean, isn't it? Legally? Yes. Morally? Not all. When I refer to morally, I'm really speaking about integrity and credibility. Do they treat their policy owners as they would like to be treated themselves? In most cases, the answer is a definitive "yes!" But, not in all cases. And, when one of own messes up, we get the heat from our policyholders. It's the old "guilt by association" syndrome!

Annuity carriers start out with the best intentions. They look at their capital, price their products for a reasonable profit, and go to market. Most companies follow the game plan, acquire more capital, increase their distribution, and become leaders in our industry. Sometimes, events beyond their control force them to make decisions that are not always well received. It's understandable. They must protect the profitability of the insurance company. After all, we sell security and you want your company to be profitable and secure. But, you don't want to be hoodwinked. You want to have a good idea as to what your client can expect in future years. Your clientele are your lifeline. They spread the word regarding your abilities. Good news travels slowly, but bad news travels fast. Guilt by association.

Some companies know they are going to "deep-six" your client's renewal rates or participation rates at the time of issue. Some companies go below their base rates in the second year. Some companies treat older policyholders differently in equity index sales when determining caps, spreads, participation rates, and fixed interest accounts. Hence, many policyholders will never "see the light of day" regarding the returns on their annuities, and they feel trapped. You are also "spread eagled" when a competitor comes behind you!

So, many states force the insurance agent to attend ethics classes. States like California want to protect the consumer from the agent. What about the insurers? I believe that the CEO's and top executives should be forced to take these classes. We are in this together!

Let's look at an example: You sell an annuity. In year two or three, renewal rates are at the guarantee. Your client is upset. You move the annuity and your client receives a barrage of conservation mail from the company insinuating that you are only doing this to make a new commission. I say that this only occurred because the company sacrificed the policy owner to increase their profits, or, in the case of the public company, attempted to drive-up or stabilize the stock price. Please allow me to reiterate: these companies are in the minority. But, they hurt your business! Now, please allow me to be blasphemous!

- There are reasons to replace annuities and life policies. There are products that can overcome surrender charges.
- There are products that will fare much better than the low guaranteed rates that your client is now experiencing.
- You do have a duty to assist your client with their retirement and life insurance dollars.
- We do have software to assist you in this venture.
- These are your clients. You brought them to the table.

I've had the wonderful experience of being a life insurance company president. I have also had the even better experience of being a life member of MDRT, CLU, and now again, owner of an Insurance Marketing Organization. I believe that the agent is the most important part of this insurance equation. You can replace CDs, you can sell your stock, you can trade in your car, you can refinance your mortgage, and you can switch your auto policy. Why is it that we feel guilty replacing policies? Because, we felt that we sold them the right one and they would perform differently than they are.

We've all told our kids since grade school: "Be careful with whom you run around. You will be judged by the <u>company</u> you keep!"

Guilt by association.

ALWAYS BE PROUD TO BE AN AGENT!

Chapter 50

Tropical Disturbance

I'm lucky to own a beachfront property in South Carolina. Lucky? As long as I remain beachfront and not washed away! That's the risk one takes when purchasing a property such as this. Many would say I'm crazy. Why take the risk? There are so many hurricanes. It's only a matter of time 'til 2nd Row becomes beachfront and my place is history. All you have to do is watch the news and it will scare the sand dollars right out of you. Right? WRONG!

Most times, it's not a hurricane. There is only a short period when hurricanes appear. We should always be prepared but we must not over react.

Here is how things start:

A tropical depression can turn into a tropical disturbance. Heavy winds and rough seas abound. It's still usually far from land. Begin to board the place up if it turns into a tropical storm. These strong winds bring about heavy rains and many times heavy flooding. Property damage comes with this occurrence. Now the big one—the hurricane. But now the big question, "where will it land; how wide a swath will it cut, and what is its "estimated time of arrival?"

We have many tropical disturbances in our lives. They appear on both personal and professional levels. Our job is to keep a keen eye on the situation, notice the symptoms and plan accordingly. A small family "tropical disturbance" can turn into a "family hurricane". That's too bad, but it does happen.

So let's prepare, have contingency plans, and go forward with our lives. Many of these storms develop beyond our control. If the worst happens—a hurricane—we must still deal with it. But don't borrow trouble. Don't assume the worst. Big ships don't get rocked ashore by small pebbles. We can always bounce back after a tragic loss. Wait a minute, isn't that why we have insurance? Insurance against dying too soon or living too long? So, walk the beach, enjoy the sounds of the surf, and bask in the sun. There is never a guarantee that you'll have this day again tomorrow.

Chapter 51

Identity Theft

According to a national business newspaper, identity theft is the fastest growing crime in America, striking over 700,000 people from all walks of life in the most recent reporting year. This startling statistic reminds us that we all need to be very careful. We do need to be careful when it comes to protecting our most private information. However, there's another kind of identity theft that affects many more people than those counted in the statistic above. As a matter of fact, this other form of identity theft has reached epidemic proportions, striking young and old, rich and poor, men and women, and people of all races and nationalities.

This "stolen" identity is *what* and *who you are*. It's your dreams and aspirations. It's what you stand for. In other words, it's what you, as a child, dreamed of becoming when you grew up. Along the way to adulthood, however, someone *stole* your identity—the who and what you are (or were to become), and you settled for something different. In some cases, you settled for less.

Now, I'm not suggesting that a career change or a different dream is bad. Heck, in many situations it may have been just what the doctor ordered. But some people, perhaps you, simply gave up and accepted their "fate" because they believed it was the right thing to do.

This kind of identity theft robs you of your heritage. It often occurs when people (or circumstances) encourage you to change your goals and settle for something of lesser value. Though financial gain may be part of the reason, I'm really not referring to income here. Doing what you really want to do often has nothing to do with how much you earn. In fact, money or financial reward may be the least important part of your identity.

The kind of shift in your life path that I'm talking about is when someone you trust, admire, or simply respect says to you, "You'll never do it!" Or, "it can't be done." Or, "don't take a chance, because you're too old (or too young, or too fat, or too tall)." These nay-sayers may even assert boldly, "You're lucky to have what you have; be thankful!" The more cynical among them may even offer, "Well, others have tried that and failed; why would you be any different?" These types of comments instill fear, create negative behavior, and cause you give up on your dreams—in essence, they help *steal* your identity!

Why would people want to steal your identity? Because, as Napoleon Hill says in his masterpiece, The Master Key to Riches, "Very few people are truly sympathetic and empathetic with your goals and desires." In other words, most people don't want you to achieve your "desired identity." When you succeed, you become a threat to them. They measure their own worth by looking at you instead of in the mirror. You make them feel bad about themselves because they recognize that they have allowed the "*theft of their own identity.*"

It's time to "check your I.D." Does it still give the proper information about you or do you need to get another card? You are more than what you do. You are the totality of your dreams and experiences, your goals and your accomplishments, your family and your friends. Unlike a stolen driver's license or social security number, you control your true identity—no one can steal from you unless you let them. So, no matter what your age or position, don't give up on your dreams—those childhood fantasies and aspirations. They are what keep us sane. Spit in the eye of the "Identity Thief"—you have something special. Don't let go of it!

Chapter 52

Life Long Learning

Ever heard the phrase "Life Long Learning" phrase before? My wife, Ann, uses it from time to time. She describes it as people of our generation and older who continue to enrich their lives through continual education. This education could be formal or informal. My wife is a perfect example of a "Life Long Learner." She reads constantly and has an interest in a variety of different topics. This makes her a more interesting person. It also makes her a person with whom people like to spend time due to her broad background. She has all of the formal education (bachelors and masters degrees), but her life experiences have had an even greater impact and influence on her "total" person.

I believe that "Life Long Learning" is extremely important in the financial services business. People rely on us for proper information and professional guidance. Our first challenge with prospects is to demonstrate that we do have the knowledge and expertise to assist them with their plans. These criteria, however, just gets us in the door. The next step is to "show our stuff." We hope that the trust is there, that our advice is sensible, and that they choose us as a member of their financial team.

So, how do we go about becoming "Life Long Learners"? There are all sorts of ways, but I'll just touch on a few of the easy ones.

First, I continue to be a strong supporter of the CLU, ChFC, and CFP designations. The curricula are well respected. And, yes, earning these designations is more time-consuming than the other designations; however, they does have meaning when you obtain them from a school, such as the American College.

Second, what about industry seminars, and how about those seminars *outside* of our comfort zone, such as seminars put on by banks, investment firms, or estate planners? This information may not be immediately applicable to your practice, but it will make you more well rounded and possibly get you additional clients.

Third, how about trade magazines? I suggest that you start reading <u>all</u> the articles (it's your *homework* assignment!). For example, read about long-term care insurance even if you don't market the product. You still need to know about it, because your clients may ask you about it! Read the daily papers, including your local paper, USA Today, and the *Wall Street Journal.* Again, we must know what our clients and prospects are reading. They will feel more comfortable with you if you are familiar with their areas of interest.

Fourth, what about the Internet? You bet! Sites such as producersweb.com and our own Ohlsongroup.com provide access to your peers and extremely valuable industry-insider information. You can pick up incredible insights into marketing, education, and research. You can obtain 10-K's of the companies you represent. How about reading a life insurance company's annual statement? It's important to know how your company is doing financially.

Finally, books—both fiction and non-fiction. I love to read history and biography. They provide insight into my life. They help me both personally and professionally. There are also great "self-help" books. They will help you "re-remember" what you may have already known. And even fiction, particularly the fiction your clients may be reading, can be helpful, if for no other reason than to give you some conversational ammunition.

In summary, you have many, many sources to turn to for "Life Long Learning"—an unlimited source, in fact. My point is, don't just think about it or talk about it—as the ad says, "Just do it!" Get involved immediately, right now. We are reminded daily about *physical* exercise, but let's not forget about our *mental* fitness. We all have long lives to live. Why not live yours while learning? I guarantee, you'll feel good about your progress, and your clients will notice the difference too!

Chapter 53

The Fruits of Their Labor

It only seems fitting, as we approach the Labor Day weekend, to pause and reflect on why we work. The answer may seem evident to you—we must work to pay for living expenses, fun, education, savings, and so forth. But, I think there are many other reasons. For example:

- We just like to work,

- We love our jobs,

- It is our way of contributing to a cause bigger than ourselves,

- To leave a legacy for our estate,

- To save for retirement, and

- Probably 100 more reasons.

But, let me get to the point. Let's forget about *us* for a moment and think about the market we serve—the SENIOR MARKET-PLACE. These people, the greatest generation, are done working. But, they are not done living. They still have concerns. Their health, their ability to have a stream of income that they cannot outlive, and their families.

I know, I know—you're saying, "there he goes again! Acting like he knows it all!" How in the heck do I know what American Seniors are thinking about? You pros are in the field. You know what their concerns are. You are doing a thorough fact finder, *aren't you?* You are reviewing their financial planning every year, *aren't you?* You are selling benefits as opposed to features, *aren't you?* You're not selling just interest rates, *are you?*

Pardon me for being cute. I do have a reason and purpose for this dialogue. Here it is! We are getting back to basics. We have been holding a series of marketing workshops in selected cities. We have been conducting follow-ups to attendees via teleconferences—live radio-style programs that bring you the latest and greatest information in our industry, with some serious heavyweights in our profession. We have developed a powerful "Toolbox For Success" with new fact finding forms, needs analysis charts, calculators, and much more. We have new seminar packages and lead generating programs, and one of the most powerful "door openers" you've ever heard of.

You see, we think it's time that we offer you more in the way of benefits versus features. In other words, *"How can we help you increase your income and enjoy your job versus a _____% commission?"*

I submit to you that you need to take the same approach with today's seniors. In other words explaining—*"What this plan will do for you"* rather than *"I can give you a rate better than a CD."*

So, we are entering an exciting period in our industry. No matter what time of year you happen to be reading this essay, consider the "Fruits of Your Labor" and why you've chosen to be in the most remarkable profession in the business world today. Remember, right after Labor Day each year, the kids are back in school, the seminar season is in full swing, tuition bills are due, and the holidays are just around the corner. There's no better time to crank up your business and get a head start on the new year!

Chapter 54

Plant Those Bulbs!

Autumn is the time of year when the days are growing shorter and it's not as comfortable walking out to get the newspaper in your bare feet. Don't get me wrong, I love the change of seasons. I always look forward to the next one!

I must admit, though, that spring and summer are my favorites. Spring brings about a rebirth of nature. It also provides me with a positive attitude towards life. Everything just looks, feels, and is better. Well, some places do look better than others. I'm now speaking of people's yards. You know what I mean. Some yards are full of beautiful flowers, lush green grass, and gorgeous trees. Some yards have my all-time favorite spring flower—the Tulip.

Now where did all of those tulips come from? Did they just appear? Well, of course not! Beautiful tulips are, in many ways, like happy families, successful businesses, good self-images, and healthy bodies. These things just don't happen. They take planning, hard work, execution, attention to detail, and a lot of caring.

Let me give you an example:

It's a Saturday in early November in Indianapolis. The temperature is about 45 degrees (about 7 degrees below normal). It's cloudy with a brisk wind, so it feels a lot colder. I'm out on my hands and knees digging little holes, inserting tulip bulbs, covering them with bone meal, and smoothing the dirt back in the hole. I can work the entire afternoon (you have to plant a LOT of Tulip bulbs), yet I still have room for more bulbs. I've now planted all the bulbs, cleaned up my mess, and I'm ready to go inside and get warm.

Before going inside, I look back to admire my work. I'm a little depressed. All that I have to show for my afternoon's effort is a sore back, scraped and dirty knuckles, a wind burned face, and bruised knees. So, why would anyone do this? I do it for SPRING!! That's when I will enjoy the bright colors, the green stems, and the beauty that it affords my home. It has to be this way—good things don't just happen. Remember, it takes planning, execution, hard work, a few bruises, and, above all else, a lot of patience. It's a lot like life itself.

Oh, I forgot one thing. This work does not always guarantee beautiful flowers (or success in life). Squirrels love to eat bulbs, dogs smell the bone meal and dig up the bulbs, and a late spring frost could damage the early growth. But, I can guarantee one thing. You will NOT have beautiful Tulips if you don't plant your bulbs in the fall. I think it is worth the risk!

So, in the fall, when planting time is about over, take the time to make your plans (plant your bulbs), and be ready to reap the rewards. Come spring you'll both be happy and sad—happy that you planted some bulbs and sad that you didn't plant more!

Chapter 55

Nonna's Kitchen Table

"Nonna" is the Italian word for grandmother. My mother is Italian, and I grew up with a lot of Italian traditions—traditions and experiences that I will treasure for the rest of my life. Most, I can never recapture and Thanksgiving is definitely one of them. Believe me, I understand that Thanksgiving is not an *Italian* holiday. But, you couldn't have sold me on that statement when I was young! I should also preface my remarks noting that every family with strong ethnic backgrounds shares these feelings.

My nonna and "nonno" (grandfather) moved to the United States with about fifty families from Northern Italy. My mother was born in Chicago, but she moved back to Italy with her mother and sister to be with the other "fatherless" families. Why were they "fatherless?" It wasn't divorce or death, but rather it was simple economics. The Great Depression of the 1930s was on, and the men traveled throughout America on trains constructing buildings for the government. Most of these Italian men were craftsmen. They were marble setters, contractors and common laborers. They worked hard, saved their money, and had their families shipped to America when World War II broke out in earnest in Italy.

Now to "Nonna's Kitchen Table." Mealtime has always been a celebration time in Italian families. It is a time to gather together, to catch up on daily events, and to engage in the Italians' favorite "sport"—ARGUING! By "arguing," I don't mean just simple disagreements discussed in level tones. No. I mean loud, pound-your-fist, turn-red-in-the-face, bellowing arguing! It's not a simple competition but a war!

In Nonna's home was one sanctuary from this "storm" where the men, especially, were not allowed—Nonna's kitchen. That was the most important spot during any Italian celebration. Italians love fine food and good wines. But those gatherings didn't just happen. To pull these off, you had to have Nonna and the rest of the women. Here is how it started.

Nonna would make homemade pasta several days before Thanksgiving. Family members would come to her house the day before to assist in the "festa." They placed the dough in a hand held pasta roller and spread it on Nonna's table. The table was eight feet long and they needed every bit of the space for the pasta preparation.

The ladies would place the ravioli filling four inches apart. Then, they would cut it in to squares and others would "tie" them up. They would do the same, in miniature form, with different fillings for the soup—the "tortellini en brodo"—(I'm starting to drool on my paper!). The major cooking began on Thanksgiving morning. If you were lucky enough to be anywhere in Nonna's home, you enjoyed the unmistakable aromas of the homemade sauce for the pasta, Italian sausages, beef roast, a huge turkey, potatoes, carrots, cranberries, fruits, cheeses, extraordinary salads, and homemade biscotti for dessert. Oh, and a great low cost Chianti for the dinner. Nonna nearly had to post a guard at the kitchen door to keep us out!

The men were in the living room talking, drinking, and smoking cigars. The kids were all running around. New babies were crying, someone may have received an occasional spanking, and the men were placing their bets on the Bears/Lions game they would watch after dinner.

At last, it was time to sit down for the meal. The crowd would be between twenty-five and forty people. No problem, even though Nonna's and Nonno's Chicago flat was only about 1500 square feet. I don't know how we all fit, but we did. We were all so excited to see each other that we probably just didn't notice the cramped quarters. I couldn't wait to see my cousins and all the others whom I thought (until I was in high school) were blood relatives.

When dinner was over, the ladies cleared the table and washed the dishes. The men crammed into the parlor to watch the football game, though in reality, most of them fell asleep. The kids, too, were starting to tire out—a wonderful end to a classic family day!

Oops! Not so fast! Something else was coming from Nonna's kitchen table—dessert and a turkey sandwich for anyone who needed that "little" something extra!

In addition to the incredible food, one ingredient made this day special—the love in everybody's hearts. Oh, they would argue and make you think that they despised each other, but it was all part of the game. They had one thing they shared for life—it's called "La Famiglia"—the family.

Thanksgiving was and is as big as Christmas for our family. It stretches over the entire weekend. In our home, we will have one hundred people over on the Friday night following Thanksgiving for what we call, appropriately, "Italian Night." Why do we do it? For the same reason you do—"La Famiglia." Nonna and her table are long gone but not her memories and the immigrant mentality that they placed in me.

Part IV

Tips: Sales & Marketing

Chapter 56

Simplicity: The Key to the Fixed Annuity Sale

Most of us came into this business hearing the famous selling tip—KISS *keep it simple, stupid.* This acronym has never been as important as it is in today's fixed annuity arena. When we speak of fixed annuities, we are addressing both the traditional fixed and the "fixed" index annuities. Let's focus for a minute on the index annuity market, which is a somewhat goofy market. Have you even seen anything like this in your insurance career? We have products that take most agents thirty minutes to understand. How are we supposed to explain them to a prospect or client in three minutes? Some agents sell index annuities like securities. Is it any surprise that regulators want to oversee this marketplace? Why are we taking such a beautiful product and making it complicated? Why are we trying to make it something it isn't? Why are some agents, and companies, trying to kill the Golden Goose? They can't help themselves. Let's examine the situation and try to make this simpler for everyone.

Index Annuities

The index annuity is a fixed annuity with a different method of crediting interest. To quote Jack Marrion, president of the Advantage Compendium,

"Fixed index annuities can best be described as savings instruments offered by insurance companies that provide a minimum guaranteed return. Insurance companies' earnings, above and beyond what is needed for this minimum guarantee, are used to purchase an index-link providing the potential for the crediting of excess interest above the minimum guarantee."

Sounds pretty simple, doesn't it? This is even better when you explain to a prospect that their principal and past interest gains are never subject to investment risk. They are backed by the faith and credit of the insurance company. This is safe and this is simple. Some might want a simple explanation of the difference between a "fixed rate" annuity and a "fixed index" annuity. Marrion continues,

"The difference between the two is that with a fixed index annuity, most of the [premiums] paid are used to buy an index-link on an equity index. This gives your client the potential for more interest if the index cooperates."

This sounds pretty simple to me. You do, of course, have the benefit of many fine point-of-sale pieces along with historical performances of each crediting methodology. So what's happened? Why all the confusion?

Many companies have made these products difficult to understand with too many index choices and too many games. Some products have stretched the surrender periods without giving anything back to the client. Don't get me wrong—long surrender periods are okay if the client gets something in exchange and fully understands what he or she is buying. Some products will never, in my opinion, perform well because they are building in unmanageable commission structures. I like high commissions as well as anyone, but not at the expense of our clients. How will we ever be able to go back on an annual review with our clients? How can we look them in the eye? Well, don't worry— changes are coming! Before we analyze potential changes, let's look at the traditional "fixed annuity."

Traditional Fixed Annuities

The traditional non-index annuity has been around for quite some time and has served a great purpose. People have been able to save money through this vehicle on a tax-deferred basis. The last ten years provided our industry with an excellent opportunity for explosive growth, and boy did it ever happen! Bank annuity sales took off; agents were experiencing tremendous increase in incomes and companies' assets exploded. The annuity design was simple: They mimicked CDs. That's the greatest benchmark for today's consumer—*"Is this annuity paying more than my CD?"* That is the most important factor in your client's decision to purchase. Tax-deferred growth, freedom from probate, and an income they can't outlive are distant "beating" the CD. But things started to get a little cloudy. Let's take a look.

Companies wanted an increase in market share. They wanted more assets under management. Remember, that's one of the two biggest factors in which an insurance company makes money. It's called the spread, or the difference between what the company earns in investment income and it pays your client. The bigger the spread, the bigger the profit. The other main factor is expense (home office costs and, of course, your commissions). So, enter the day of the first year bonus. This "sizzling" first-year rate brought in a lot of money. These bonuses have brought about some criticism from the press as well as disgruntled clients. Why? Renewal rates, in many cases, tanked. These were declared rate annuities that allowed the company to "declare" where they set the renewal rates. Many companies in search of income reduced your client's rate to increase the spread. Wall Street liked it, but not the policyholder. I believe that it's in your best interest, as well as your clients', to purchase a multi-year rate guaranteed annuity if you are not proposing an index annuity. Otherwise, your client is saving in a vehicle with no guarantee of future results. They surely wouldn't do this with a bank CD. Don't get me wrong; there are plenty of honorable companies that will treat your client fairly. Also, we do want the company to be profitable, since it is your partner. There are many ways to analyze a company to determine how they will renew your clients' rates.

- Make sure they have plenty of capital and/or strong reinsurers.
- Review its annual statement to see if it is making money.
- Check to see if it has been selling off its portfolio to take investment gains. If it has, it probably reinvested at lower rates, which reduce its spread (profit). It may reduce rates to increase that spread.

- Ask to take a look at their past renewals. History is not always an indication of the future but could prove to be a guide.

I have been fortunate to be on both sides of the fence. I've been an insurance company president as well as spending twenty-plus years in the field as an agent, general agent, and owner of an insurance marketing organization. So, please excuse me if I tend to overanalyze. But, I am happy to say that the next couple of years will get our annuity industry back on track.

Companies are now designing new products, pulling old products, and adhering to new regulatory guidelines. The business is going to be better than ever! The policyholder, the insurance company, and the agent will all do well! We are getting back to a level playing field. I, for one, am extremely happy with the direction our industry must take if we are going to be able to operate profitably without government intervention. So, what do we do next?

Here we go:

- Sell only what you believe in. Don't rationalize away parts of the contract you don't like.
- Only sell "GOOD STUFF". Have a concise presentation that provides your prospect or client with all the information they need to make a decision. They buy easier when they understand what you are selling.
- Don't over promise.
- Don't sell the stock market. This isn't an investment.

The fixed index annuity is the most important annuity in the industry. Seniors and boomers will continue to buy. Our future is bright for multiple sales of annuities and ancillary products—but only if our clients are happy with previous purchases. This product is simple and beautiful. Sell it properly and you will profit immensely. The answer is simple. *Sell it right and sell what's good for everyone.*

We can't lose.

Chapter 57

Come Together

We had a great meeting last week. We invited some of our associates around the country to come in for a "brainstorming session." These people do business in Michigan, Ohio, North Carolina, South Carolina, Indiana, Tennessee, Illinois, and elsewhere. They are great personal producers in their own right, but they also have agents they have recruited. They provide training, marketing support, seminar systems, niche marketing, and back-office support. Their biggest concern is to make sure that their field associates prosper, not only now but into the future. That's why we were meeting.

Let me explain.

It would be an understatement to say that the industry is going through great change. But, frankly, "you ain't seen nothing yet!" Marketing expertise, availability to research, and beneficial education will be a few of the factors that will be of paramount importance to our careers. But who is going to provide these three elements to us in the field? The insurance companies? Think again. It's up to you and me. That is why we came together for this meeting—to best determine how we will offer top notch support in all areas to you the producer. Remember, you are our most valuable asset. The meeting was successful!

Here's what we determined.

FIRST, synergism is key. In other words, one plus one can equal *three*.

SECOND, we can hang by ourselves or we can hang together.

THIRD, there is strength in numbers.

FOURTH, each of us has different skills and strengths.

So, we came together for the start of a very serious strategic alliance: successful professionals specializing in life, health, LTC, Med Supp, annuities, financial institution, marketing, and more. We believe we can be of greater value to you, our field associates, when we pool the resources of this strategic alliance. We know, without any doubt, that everyone will win!

These are serious times with serious opportunities for serious people. The exchange of ideas and information, coupled with unique industry experiences, will provide greater benefit to our industry associations. Each of these organizations maintains their own independence and ownership, but, they are committed to the success of each of the members. We are actually pursuing proprietary products through various insurance companies and product design changes that will allow the agent to participate in the profitability of the products he or she sells.

These are truly great times. I love the upheaval and uncertainty in our industry. These are the times when great ideas flourish. If you are already part of our group, thanks so much. If not, give us a call! It's time to COME TOGETHER!

Chapter 58

Past Performance

We all seem to spend some time focusing on past performance when we make a purchase. Today, there is greater access to information regarding this topic—the Internet. For instance, you can go online to check the resale value of a car model you are contemplating purchasing. It's simple to go to the appropriate website, plug in the model, answer a few questions, and bingo, there is the range of pricing.

The same thing holds true with appliances. You can determine the number of complaints, *Consumer Report* ratings, and the approximate cost of energy use over time. The same holds true for prescription drugs, airlines with the fewest flight delays, cars with the lowest insurance rates, colleges ranked by various news magazines, wines by various wine magazines, retirement homes ranked by the lowest income tax, legislation passed by political parties, and much more. But, there is a stronger benchmark for past performance. That factor is personal experience.

Here we go.

I was fortunate, early in my career, to attend two weeks of training (nobody would sit for two weeks today!) in a course called Modelnetics™. It was a division of Main Event Management™. The course is still around today. It broke management down into 150 models. One of the models was the "connoisseur affect". Simply put, it stated that, "People judge things by the best and the worst that they have experienced." I believe that remains true today.

I had dinner with my parents last evening. They commented that they were probably going to have to purchase a new refrigerator. Their current *GE* unit is twenty years old and has served them well. They are not going to shop around. They are not going to *Consumer Reports,* and they definitely are not going online to investigate. Why? They are going to buy another GE. It has served them well and they won't switch. They are even buying from the same appliance store. I suggested that they look at *Best Buy, Home Depot,* or some other large vendor.

"No way!" they shouted. Why? The appliance store has always treated and served them well. The last time they purchased an item from a large discount store, they didn't get good service at repair time. So, my folks represent an excellent example of the connoisseur effect. They judge things by the best and worst experiences they've had. There are many similarities to our financial services professions.

By the way, please note that I refer to our career as a "profession." A profession entails building future relationships and business. It also means being the "go to guy or gal." Hence, the word *profession,* which begets the word "professional". Too many of our prospects, primarily in the senior market, have dealt with fast talking, quick hit, "sales people"—you know them—the ones who promise their clients the world and are never to be found when the client needs attention.

Oh, I used the word "client." Only a professional has clients. A "salesperson" has customers. I should probably say "one-sale customers!" That's not what our profession is built upon and not what our clients want. They deserve someone who will listen to their desires, needs, wants, and goals. They deserve someone who will listen to their fears, special needs, challenges, and concerns. They are not looking for quick fixes, stories too good to be true, or products that don't stand a chance of delivering what the "sales person" has promised. Clients simply want someone to talk to—someone they can trust, someone who will ease their concerns and calm their fears. That someone should be you, the professional advisor. What a business and what an opportunity we have. Wait! I should say, what a profession!

So, here we are back to past performance. How do we exhibit our past performance? There are many ways.

- First, how about written testimonials from your clients?
- Second, how about a complaint-free Better Business Bureau (BBB) standing?
- Third, how about the length of time you have been in this great business?
- Finally, what about your commitment to the community through volunteer efforts?

"But," you ask, "what about the products we offer?"
Please indulge me one more time.
I am now addressing the "fixed or guaranteed" side of our indus-

try. Variable and securities professionals have a little more, but not much, leeway. Don't over-promise. Those 3% monthly caps will not get your client a 36% return. You don't believe it and neither do they. So, what about taking the crediting methodology of an EIA, fill in the requested surrender period, link it to the index you are using, and show an actual historical return. I know that past performance is no indication of future growth, but it does show the past. It's not unlike the *Kelly Blue Book* or *Consumer Reports* or other sources for past performance of automobiles.

Compare annuities to CDs. Compare the tax-free estate building benefits of life insurance to the other financial products. Compare disability income to a "pay out of your pocket plan." You get the picture? Bottom line: if this is a profession to you, then you are building past performance for your future. Don't make promises that you can't keep. Over-deliver; believe in your products, do the right thing, and your successful future is guaranteed—absolutely!

Chapter 59

"I Need Your Help!"

Have you ever heard those words before? Have you ever said these words before? I'm sure that you've answered, "yes" to at least one if not both of these questions. Many people have a difficult time asking for help. Why? What's the deal? Do some people perceive it as a weakness? Does it imply the person cannot handle things on his/her own? Some people undoubtedly believe that there's nothing anyone else can do to help or that people don't or won't want to help. I believe that is dead wrong. Allow me to explain.

I'm writing this essay around the anniversary of 9/11. That unforgettable day, and events surrounding it, has provided me with hope and contentment. I know you must have just blinked! "Did he just say, 'contentment' from 9/11?" Let me explain.

The American and international communities exhibited an unbelievable amount of caring and help after the terrorist attack. Significantly, people offered help <u>before</u> they were asked. People simply said, "how can I help?" That gives me contentment and hope.

We don't need to rehash the events of that horrible day. All of us have the terrible images burned into our minds, permanently. But the outpouring of goodness, strength, and humility was unbelievable. It showed the world what the American spirit means. It also confirmed that we are a nation of helpers—that we Americans will "step up to the plate" even when we aren't called to do. That's why I've never been afraid to say, "I need your help."

Now, in our financial services business, if we are to believe all the trade journals, card packs, email blasts, and teleconferences each of us must do seminars to succeed in our business. We must have a new, high-powered, "never-seen-before-widget" to make it big! How many ads have you seen that proclaim:

"We are the best!" "Our seminar guarantees you will be the best!" "Hear are our $10 million producers—you could be one of them!" Or, *"You can't win without our ammo!"*

PHOOEY!

OK. I <u>do</u> believe in seminar and workshops for those who like them and can do them effectively. But what about some 'secret weapon' that may fill up your appointment schedule? This is designed for producers who would rather deal "one on one." This is for financial planners who are wondering, "how do I jump-start my business today?" The answer is simply, "believe in people's desire to help."

Let's get started.

1. Repeat after me: "I NEED YOUR HELP." Now, that wasn't too bad was it?
2. Put together a list of your best clients.
3. Call and invite them to lunch or breakfast. The breakfast appears to be an overlooked meeting time. The senior gets up early. Yes, we are buying food again. But, wouldn't you pay for a stranger's meal at your seminar/workshop?
4. Advise your client that nothing will be sold at the lunch/breakfast. You wish to review, discuss, and get up to date on their financial situation. You will also give them some new ideas and update them on saving, rates, and tax law changes.
5. At the meal, be sure to bring ideas! Uncover new needs and sales possibilities with your client and set up a follow-up appointment if the situation is right.
6. <u>Now, for the secret weapon</u>. You open your mouth, sit up straight, look your client in the eye, and say, "I need your help." Let your client know that you need new quality prospects, just like them. Advise them that you need <u>at least</u> three good names. That's right; be specific!
7. Then, ask them to call these new prospects in advance to alert them to your forthcoming call.

Secret weapon? No, this is Selling 101. This is not a secret power point presentation, special mailer, advanced training course, or magic beads. This is simply trusting people and asking for their help. You spent a lot of time and money getting the first sale from your client. Go back, review, get referrals, and try to sell more. Repeat business and new clients are the lifelines of your financial practice. I hope this helps.

Oh by the way, do you have another minute or two? I NEED YOUR HELP!! I NEED YOUR BUSINESS!! I NEED AGENTS

REFERRED TO ME!! I need to know what you want. Please call us today. What will we talk about?

A) Review what you sell, who you sell through, who you sell to and why.

B) I'll advise you of our products and services guarantee that we will <u>care</u> and do what we can to <u>help you</u>!

C) I'll ask for the opportunity to earn your business and ask for names of other agents that could use my help.

In summary, let's help each other. Why not? We are in it together.

Chapter 60

Making the Sale…but not the commission!

An all too common situation in the financial services business is making the sale but NOT the commission—a very disappointing development. We line up a sales appointment, strut our stuff, tell all we know, go for the close, and the client says, "I need a little time to think it over!"

It's understandable when this happens once in awhile, but it is not acceptable if it becomes the norm. What goes wrong in this type of situation? Where are we making our mistakes? Are we just setting the table for a competitor to come in behind us, benefit from our knowledgeable presentation, and make the sale? It's happened to me and I didn't like it. I'm sure you don't either. So, let's remedy this situation.

First, we need to remember <u>why</u> we are at the appointment. No matter how you slice, the reason we make appointments with a client is to consummate a deal. Sure, we should teach and explain, but we must not get into lateral conversations regarding financial issues that are of no concern to the prospect.

Second, we need to listen to our prospects. Find out what their greatest financial concerns are today. We need to ask probing questions—leading questions. Remember, your clients are meeting with you because you have demonstrated to them that you have a prescription that can cure a financial disease.

Third, we should isolate the need. We continue to focus on the problem, but we don't give the solution at this time.

Fourth, we should try to get the prospect to agree that there <u>is</u> a problem and get him/her to voice his/her feelings about rectifying the situation.

Fifth, and finally, we propose the solution—the solution to the isolated need only. Many producers fail at this point by talking too much, by strutting their stuff, and showing off. Don't fall into that trap.

When you have the sale consummated, don't start expounding on all you know. You will just confuse the prospect, take his eye off the ball, and cause a delay in the decision making process.

Sixth, you must close the sale. Be <u>friendly, fair, firm</u> and <u>frank</u>! You've read all of the books, attended all of the seminars on selling and closing, and have had years of experience—now is the time to DO IT! Ask for the order. Get a signed contract. Pick up a check.

Nearly as important is the seventh step—get referrals from your client. You've just made the sale. You have won a new friend and customer. It just makes sense that this person would be a great source of new sales leads for you. So, be sure to ask!

Remember, a free-wheeling presentation makes it difficult to focus on the need at hand. It will set the table for a competitor to come in behind you, reorganize your presentation, find your client's hot button, and collect <u>your</u> commission dollars! It's too hard getting qualified prospects! Seminars are expensive if you are not making sales. They are inexpensive (cheap!) if you're capitalizing on your audience and understanding the sales process.

NEED HELP? Call us! That's our primary job—making sure you make the sale and GET THE COMMISSION TOO! Good selling.

Chapter 61

Autopilot

Language is, at best, symbolic behavior. The words we use symbolize meaning that is often foreign to those around us. On the other hand, we sometimes use words that we think we know the meaning of, but in fact, we don't. For example, we've all heard the expression "running on autopilot" many times. It was originally used to describe a flight situation. A pilot would chart a course via radar, load the final destination, and the plane would automatically follow the instructions. The use of computers today makes this task even easier.

Passengers usually feel more comfortable in an autopilot situation when the visibility is bad due to inclement weather. But what most of us don't realize is that the pilots are not taking a snooze during this "automatic" control situation. On the contrary, the pilots are constantly checking their instruments: the dials, levers, air pressure, altitude, and all of the other intricate details of being a professional pilot. In short, they are <u>fully aware</u> of what's going on!

As with much jargon today, many of us have adopted the term "autopilot" and are using it to describe our lives, jobs, or families—often, <u>erroneously</u>. For example, someone asks, "How's your job going?" Your response, "Great! It's on autopilot!" Simple, right? Wrong! Unlike the pilot who is paying close attention even when flying on autopilot, many of us are paying little if any attention to what's going on around us, thinking that we're on "autopilot" and everything is fine. And that's bad.

Things are changing rapidly in today's world. All you have to do is pick up a newspaper, listen to the radio, or watch the news on TV. You may get more information than you want, but how do you process and use this information? I believe that we process the information that affects our personal lives in greater detail than we do the information that can affect our business lives. We think we're on autopilot, but we're <u>not</u> really paying attention. Here are a few examples:

At the time of this writing, Flu vaccines are in short supply. The health services organization is suggesting that anyone who is in an at-risk group needs to be first for flu shots. This decision makes the rest of us anxious; we process the information and deal with the situation at hand by making plans.

Here's another example. A couple of our major airlines are either in bankruptcy or preparing to file. Much has been written regarding the fate of our "frequent flyer miles". What should we do? Well, we heard the news, processed it and acted upon the information. We may have booked flights before the flyer miles expire or transferred them to another account.

What about the war on terror? Have we processed this information? You bet! Overseas travel was, and still is, down. Rooms in Madrid are at an all time low. Flights to the Middle East are at giveaway fares. Evidently, many of us received the information, processed it, and acted—by NOT flying to hot spots. So, where am I going with this?

Just like our personal lives, we had better not put our business lives on autopilot. Allow me to be more emphatic: please don't ever say that your business is on autopilot! To do so indicates that you are "UNAWARE OF WHAT'S HAPPENING IN THE WORLD AROUND YOU!" And, I know that's not the case. At least, it shouldn't be.

Let's look at a few newsworthy items that have occurred, or may occur, that can significantly affect our business and our financial lives. (This list can be huge, so I will just mention a few and have you think about the repercussions.)

- Do Not Call List
- Do Not Fax List (currently under review-scheduled to go into affect Spring 2005)
- Spam Rules and Regulation
- New suitability rules (causes the elimination of many long surrender products)
- Proposed new SPIA Regulation (allows the first $20,000 in insurance to be tax free or at a lower rate)
- SB620 (do I need say more?)
- Eventual elimination of the federal estate tax
- Potential increase in taxes on income over $200,000 (how will this affect all of you who are sub-chapter S corps?)

- New Recovery Rules in states (Medicaid planning)
- New non-resident continuing education requirements
- Catch-up provisions on qualified plans
- Underwritten SPIAs
- Average nursing home cost
- Up to $100,000 deduction for 6,000lb cars/trucks

Ok, enough is enough! My point is this—keep a keen ear and a sharp eye on what's going on around you. It's great when things are running smoothly and we refer to it as running on "autopilot." It seems like nothing could go wrong—we must then be extra observant of our surroundings and have a plan for the worst (ask our associates in Florida if the horrible weather in the fall of 2004 affected their businesses). Be the good pilot. Continue to check your charts and dials. And finally, check in with the "observation deck and tower" (The Ohlson Group in Indianapolis!) from time to time. We have all of the information that you need to have an enjoyable flight and a safe landing!

Chapter 62

You Can Bank On It

A recent report stated, "Fixed annuities sold by banks jumped to $18.8 billion in the first half of the year, up 70% from last year." WOW! What a jump! Also, independent agents and banks account for approximately 75% of the fixed annuity business. So, what does all of this mean?

1. Fixed annuities are in vogue.
2. Our "former competitors" are now selling the fixed product.
3. Stock brokers are now pushing the fixed product to stabilize their client's portfolios.
4. Public awareness is now high regarding fixed annuities (full page article in USA Today).
5. People's 401(k)s and IRAs have reduced in value and they are looking for a "safety net".
6. This _will be_ the greatest decade for fixed annuities!

Now, what should we do?

- Set up alliances with small- to mid-sized community banks, savings & loans and credit unions.
- Differentiate yourself from the competitors with your care and product knowledge.
- Understand fully the unique characteristics of the annuity and how it may preserve family income in the future. (Check individual state laws)
- Promote yourself as a professional in this arena.
- Start a "tip club" once per month. Enlist CPAs, elder law attorneys, bankers, and trust officers—exchange ideas and leads.
- Finally, "SELL LIKE HELL". Don't look back with regrets. People want what you have, appreciate "one on one counseling," and are willing to give referrals.

So, take it to the bank! But, leave a little behind to invest in your business. Can you find a better return? I don't think so!

Chapter 63

"Reach Out and Touch Someone"

The concept of "reaching out and touching someone" via tele-marketing, in particular, is becoming more difficult in the financial services business. New watchdogs are overseeing how every business is soliciting new business. In some states, California in particular, it's even difficult to contact current clients, i.e., people with whom you've already established a relationship. Financial services advisors are not the only people feeling this new "pain." The insurance companies are as well. What effect will these new regulations have on new business development and profitability for the companies and producers? What are the areas with which all of us should be concerned?

First, we are dealing with the federal "Do Not Call List" rules. A producer must make sure that his/her list is "scrubbed"—all Do Not Call individuals removed from his or her lists. Second, what about current clients? Can they be called? The answer is only if you have conducted business during a certain period of time (most regulations require within the past eighteen months). Will this affect an insurance company's ability to cross market their existing policyholders? So, make sure you have a process in place to protect yourself.

Next, the government has recently been tightening the restrictions (cracking down) on lead cards and advertisements used to sell senior products. The regulators want us to eliminate many specific words in our marketing materials. For example, these words or phrases include, but are not limited to, "Medicare and Social Security." The regulators are also looking at the print style and typeface size (font size)—an area that is sure to garner additional attention.

And, how about the "big one"—SB620 in California? You need a Navajo guide and a road map to get through this bill! California is taking the position that a 65-year-old cannot protect him or herself from the financial services advisor. Maybe, the 65-year-old should be more afraid of SB620 and the service limitations that accompany it.

In summary, the advisor and the companies are in this together.

This isn't a time to bury our heads in the sand. We live in a very litigious society. People don't just sue one person or entity. They go all the way up the food chain. What's a person to do? Make sure you are dealing with experts who can help keep you out of harm's way and help you develop your plan to increase profitability.

That's why The Ohlson Group is here. That's what we do for you, for our industry, and for ourselves. We stay on top of all of the regulations and laws as they change (seemingly daily) to help you stay on the right side of the equation and earn even higher profits from your efforts!

Chapter 64

The "Junior" Seniors

They're all around you. The author of this article is one of "them". Who are these people? They are today's baby boomers. They will be fueling the financial services industry for many years to come. Many in this group are your friends, neighbors, fellow club members, members of your place of worship, and vendors to you. This group, primarily in their 50's, has a great need for your services today. You don't have to wait until they are 65 plus to begin working with their retirement needs and opportunities.

Much has been written about the trillions (that's right, there is a "t" at the beginning of that word) of dollars that will be passed down from the senior generation to boomers. I believe that we are making a grave mistake if we wait around for things to happen. There are ways to integrate this market into your "senior" practice today without disrupting your business.

Let's examine the characteristics of this "baby-boomer" market. They're hard workers, entrepreneurial, and living the good life. Many were the first generation to graduate from college. They want even better things for their children. The grandchildren of this group will be the "apple of their eyes." Many in this group have worked jobs since they were freshman in high school. They rewarded themselves in their adult lives with nice homes, cars, clothes, vacations, and much more. They spend a lot of money. They are concerned about retirement. They are just not sure when they will retire. Some will inherit great sums of money. They will need help in putting these funds to work. Some had kids later in life. They will need life insurance for a longer period. May have placed their parents in a nursing home. They will be interested in long term care. And, many lost a large percentage of their nest egg in the stock market crash. They waited for the market to come back and are now more cautious.

Summary, they are excellent candidates for equity index annuities and single premium life. The problem is, that no one is offering these products to them. They are a forgotten group. Oh sure, many have good life agents and financial planners assisting them with other needs—but, many have traded securities online, bought cheap term through ads and have believed that they could manage their finances as good as anyone. NOT ANYMORE! They've been financially spanked—time for us to come to the rescue! Ok, how?

1. Go to your client's kids. What a natural market.
2. Try a new mailing approach. Identify the problems and propose a meeting to offer solutions.
3. Ads in suburban papers. Costs are lower and boomers live in 'bedroom' communities.

This article was not to give you the 'silver bullet' to conquer this market. It's to get us thinking about the potential that lies ahead. Will this be the "Email Marketing Approach" that we've been waiting for? Think about it—low cost, fast, no stamps and they don't have to take the time for a free lunch or dinner.

- I am one of these boomers.
- I am *never* called on by an insurance agent.
- I am *never* called on by a financial planners.
- I *do* get cold calls from stock brokers in New York.
- I *don't* get direct mail addressing my needs.

So, the market is open. Be like a farmer—plant your seeds today and hope for a great harvest tomorrow.

Chapter 65

The Spoken Word

Ever heard the old saying, "It's not what you say but how you say it?" Believe me, I have in my thirty years of a great marriage. My wife also reminds me to "quit selling" when I try to work my way out of an "inappropriate statement."

So many statements can be misinterpreted that we may only have one chance, in the senior market especially, to make our point. What is our (your) most important point? I believe it is that you can be trusted. I think it also is the fact that you will explain things to your senior clients' satisfaction.

Here's an example; I don't think the senior client wants a graduate course or long explanation as to the role that option purchases play in an equity index annuity. Oh, they are polite people, and they will listen, but the deal is off the table. As I mentioned early in this book, the KISS method is still the best. This is not meant to be disrespectful, but the senior client is not looking for complicated deals or concepts. They've heard it all and know when it sounds to good to be true.

So what do we want to convey? Why not ask them? How about: "I assume that preserving and protecting your capital is most important. Am I correct? I also assume that a reasonable rate of return, one that will beat inflation, is more important than risking your principal for a 'home run' return. Am I correct?"

These are just a few possible approaches. You are the expert and can do better than I can. Keep your clients' money safe. Give them liquidity, an income they can't outlive, and speak to them like you'd like your parents to be spoken to.

I also always remember what my Italian nonna (grandmother) used to remind me, "Raymond, you were born with two ears and one mouth. So you're supposed to do twice as much listening." So with that, I'll take her advice. I'd love to read your thoughts.

Chapter 66

Too Much Information!

That may be an understatement! There are so many choices available to the consumer today. There are scores of rating agencies, rating magazines, and "Blue Ribbon" Award firms. The internet can provide you with more facts than you desire. I believe that this is what they mean when they refer to information overload.

So what are the most important factors that assist a consumer in making a purchase? There are many, but the most important, single factor is <u>trust</u>—belief and confidence in the product and/or the representative offering the merchandise. It's surely true in the financial services industry. The prospect "sizes you up." He or she has either met with you "one on one" or became acquaintanced with you and your firm via a seminar. They have:

- formed a first impression,
- listened to "how" you say what you say, and
- seen your product presentation.

Nonetheless, most sales are made by first earning your client's trust and confidence.

Advertisements can be a big help in building your <u>brand</u>. Time in the business is a big help. Community activities are always a plus. But, in the end, it's "do they feel confident dealing with you?" If they do and have a need for your products and services, you will probably make the sale.

So, spend more time asking your prospects what he or she lilkes or dislikes. Show a keen and sincere interest in their lives and goals. Treat them with the same dignity and respect that you would expect were you the client. People want to believe. They want to trust. They want peace of mind. You are there to deliver all of this and more!

By the way, I "trust" that <u>you</u> will have "confidence" in our ability to assist you with your "needs." We are ready to listen and are truly interested in your success!

Chapter 67

Use The Press

A *USA Today* article in an issue of our e-newsletter, *The Ohlson* Report, provided some positive information relative to our profession. It was refreshing to see an article in the general media that was not "bashing" our products. Over the years, the press has really trashed variable annuities, for example. This article happened to speak to the strengths of the product. Oh yes, it spoke of the high commissions and other <u>perceived</u> negatives, but the strengths of the product in this article, far outweighed the weaknesses. When discussing your products in light of somewhat negative or even erroneous publicity, take a positive approach. Here's an example:

- Yes, Mr. Prospect, reinvested dividends are not included in your potential return in an EIA. If they were, the past 40 years averaged a 10.4% return (wow—at 10% money doubles in 7 years).
- But, without dividends, that past 40 year average was 6.8% (money doubles in 10.5 years).
- Participation rates? "My company has a minimum floor..."
- Withdrawals? 10% per year, much more (or 100%) if in a nursing home and you are already over or close to age 59?, so don't sweat that.
- Financial Strength? We are in luck—my carriers have very strong ratings!
- Regulation? Who's been dealing with the big problems? The SEC and NASD (mutual fund scandals, fictitious earnings, variable earnings, pay telephones and others)? Or the individual insurance departments? We look pretty good.
- Potential for losses? If you withdraw earnings, you could lose money. That would be your choice, Mr. Prospect. Bottom line, you can't lose if you stay in. Taxes? Withdrawals from annuities are taxed as income, gains from S&P index fund taxed at lower cap gains tax.
- Maybe. You're earned income tax rate may be lower than cap gains.

- You may want to annuitize and spread out the taxes. Or, if it's a Medicaid friendly annuity, you may just keep money that the government would otherwise take.

Bottom line: the best defense is a good offense. Use the press to your benefit. Your clients and prospects will be glad you explained the product. It's much better when <u>you</u>, the professional, do it rather than their next door neighbor!

Chapter 68

All Business Is Show Business

Ever wonder why a prospect or client doesn't jump at the proposal you've just presented? The idea seems so logical and perfect for your client, yet he or she doesn't take action. You may go back to the office and write it off as a "bad prospect," and that may, in fact, be the case. Or, it may be that you didn't set the stage properly. Allow me to explain.

All people who are called upon to be persuasive must prepare their audience. This is true of teachers, physicians, men of the cloth, parents, politicians, and, yes, even financial services sales people. They must do the following:

1) Get their prospects/customers to like them;
2) try to establish a feeling of trust or mutual respect; and
3) convince the client to view you as a knowledgeable expert in your field.

How about some examples:

A) Letterman and Leno warm up with a monologue. The success, or lack thereof, of this presentation will probably determine if you, watching at home, will stay with them or channel surf.
B) Weekly Worship Services—the opening of a sermon will probably dictate your level of interest. Interaction with the congregation, good eye contact, and the message delivered in an understandable fashion have the best chances of "getting through" to the masses.
C) The physician has a professional staff, his credentials on the wall, and a desire to listen. This is the medical doctor whose advice you are likely to adhere to. The doctor who has his hand on the door, takes other calls, and shows lack of interest does not instill great confidence on a "pre-surgery" visit.
D) The good politician is "well-schooled" in his or her speeches. He or she wears suitable clothing, uses appropriate gestures, and has done adequate research in bringing a message that you might just get passionate about.

Setting the stage means preparing the client or prospect for the "show"—your presentation. It includes everything you have at your disposal: your appearance, voice, knowledge, materials, personality, and sincerity. It is NOT an act, though it is "acting"—you are playing the role of financial planning expert, and just like a good actor, you must be believable. Here are some tips. These ideas work in a "one on one" situation or in a seminar setting:

1) Take the Boy Scout Oath and "be prepared!" Know your stuff, look and sound the part, and be organized!
2) See the sale being made in your "minds eye."
3) Coax your client into conversations that prompt him or her to speak. Stay away from questions that only demand a yes/no answer. Engage your prospect in the transaction.
4) Focus on their top priorities. Eliminate their most bothersome worries.
5) Sell benefits, not the features. And, speak in terms they can understand and relate to.
6) Treat them with the same dignity and respect that you would desire if the tables were reversed.
7) Ask for questions or objections. If none, dig some up. You know they have some.
8) Isolate objections and answer to their satisfaction.
9) Review the product, get agreement on the solution, and invoke from them a desire to take action.
10) Ask for the order.
11) Be prepared to answer additional objections.
12) Close.
13) Thank and congratulate and get referrals.

Seems simple, right? It's a lot easier if you set the stage properly. A good performance will lead your client to direct other people to you. People want to feel good and informed. You are on stage! Give them what they want and we all win.

Chapter 69

Baby Boomer Inheritance— Fact or Fiction?

We've been hearing and reading about the trillions of dollars that will pass from today's retirees to their children in the form of inheritance. Some baby boomers feel very comfortable knowing that Mom & Dad are going to pass down a "boatload of dough" at their passing—of course, the boomers want their parents to live a very long life, but feel sure that there will still be a significant amount left behind. Don't be so sure! I don't believe that it will be nearly as significant as some would have you believe. Let's examine.

I agree, today's retirees are one of the wealthiest segments of our society. No other generation has accumulated this much money! These are some of the hardest working, most industrious and most frugal group of people that the world has ever seen.

The Greatest Generation, as Tom Brokaw describes them in the title of his book, are also living longer. Medical breakthroughs, access to care, less stress, greater physical activity and better diets are having these people living into their 80s and 90s. That's great because, for the most part, they are able to enjoy their lives. But, they have to spend part of the kids' inheritance to live. You see, fifteen to twenty years ago, economists figured that these people would die much sooner and would use less of the Social Security Dollars. That's not happening. In fact, boomers are going to wait a little longer to get their Social Security income and it may be less. So, what's a boomer to do? SAVE! SAVE! SAVE!

Let's investigate:

Now, I believe that there is a big difference between your savings and your investment dollars. Savings money is money where your principle is free from risk and your return is moderate. Hopefully, there is a tax advantage to this instrument.

Investments on the other hand, involve risk. That's fine. Analyze the risk/reward calculation and place your money in an investment that will give you an opportunity to take part in the potential growth of stocks or mutual funds. I think that this must be a big part of the baby boomers portfolio. But how do you determine the percentages to be placed in each account. Let's examine:

FIRST, they are hopefully dealing with advisors that can assist the boomer in properly allocating money into savings and investments. But, what if your client wants a quick answer that will at least be safe? Try this one (this goes back to early securities and insurance training):

1) How long will the boomer live?   *Let's say 85 years.*
2) How old is he now?   *52 years old.*
3) Subtract and you get   *33*

Put 33% in aggressive investments. Put the balance of 67% in more savings oriented vehicles.

Isn't it nice that index annuities and enhanced guarantee annuities give your client a "safe" savings haven with upside potential?

Know any boomers? Call them up. They are the new Senior Generation. Fill them in on the facts. Help them fill the void between inheritance and retirement income.

Chapter 70

Customer Loyalty

Customer loyalty. Much has been written about this subject, but unfortunately, not much has been accomplished. We seem to live in a "special offer" world. There are coupons, discounts, preferred customer days, fire sales, and more to get business. The financial services industry seems to be following in the footsteps of other industries. Producers/advisors are spending unbelievable amounts of money to attract new prospects. The hope, of course, is to turn them into clients. Insurance companies and, to a lesser extent, marketing organizations are much the same. Recently, I've seen "fire sales," premium bonuses, summertime "sizzlers," on commissions, and additional perks offered to push the product. The hopes are that you will write business with the marketing organizations and the companies to help them finish strong for the year. But what about agent/advisor loyalty? Are the marketing organizations and insurance companies really fostering this concept?

The cost of acquiring a new client, or agent, in my case, is very high. We are all going after the same demographic groups with similar products from similar companies. We are all promising topnotch service, integrity, business acumen, and ideas that will explode in people's minds. We are hopeful that we made a great first impression, caught the client/agent in a time of need, offered a product that hit their hot button, and that we ultimately did business. Lot's of work…very expensive, and we are back at it tomorrow. Like gerbils on a treadmill! So, what are we supposed to do? This is tough work. I've got a crazy idea. How about trying this?

We tell our clients/agents that we need their help. We let them know that we want to do more than sell them one policy. We promise topnotch service, and we really deliver. We call our clients/agents on a regular basis to just "check in." We become team members. We ask for referrals. We let the client/agent know that we want to do "total account development" with them. In other words, we want to earn their loyalty!

What a concept, but we can't just expect it to happen. We have to <u>make</u> it happen. It is at this moment our customers turn into clients. This is the time when agents turn into associates. We all need each other. Life is more fun when we work together on a common cause. So, let's start helping our clients/agents and they may start helping us.

I don't know about you, but I would rather work with fewer clients as opposed to a lot of customers. I am working on earning our agents/associates loyalty. Are you earning your client's loyalty?

Chapter 71

An Easier Way To Break Into Group Sales

You might be like many agents who send out letters to business owners asking for the opportunity to quote their group life and health programs. In the letter, you highlight your experience and successes while promising to give them an unbiased assessment and a quote on their present coverage. You also mention that you are an independent; therefore, you are free to use the best carrier. You assure the owner that *he or she* would be your client, not the insurance company.

Since the rising cost of health insurance is on the minds of all business owners, both large and small, you might mention new plan changes, HSAs, or some other approach that could lead to a reduced premium for the employer. You then follow up with a phone call. You summarize the contents of your letter and ask the business owner for an appointment. Although this approach may sound quite basic, in reality, the employee benefit/corporate market is one of the toughest to get started in.

The method I've just described is not always successful. In fact, more and more these days, it is usually unsuccessful in getting an appointment. Is there any easier, more effective way to get your foot in the door?

Most businesses have three critical areas of concern or "hot buttons": If you "lead" with these ideas in mind, you stand a far better chance of getting an appointment.

1. They need new customers to get increased profits—new sales are their lifeblood.
2. They need to keep existing customers happy and buying more—this reduces overall cost and drives profits.
3. They need quality employees. Employees are the backbone of every organization—without good employees, most businesses are dead in the water. The owner has invested a significant

amount of time, money, and manpower into developing these key players and doesn't want them to leave. Retention is key.

Let's address these hot buttons using a new approach.

- Prior to making any sales calls, develop a strategic alliance with a group insurance specialist. Let this specialist know that you will call him or her in when needed. Now you have an expert on your team.
- Next, assemble your owner prospect list, but prepare a new message. Introduce yourself *as a specialist in employee benefits* communication *and voluntary benefits*. Ask for fifteen minutes to describe your services. Assure the prospect that you don't want to sell them anything. Tell them to put the checkbook in the safe.
- If you sound sincere, you'll probably secure an appointment. Next, return to the hot buttons. Advise the owner that many of his or her employees don't truly understand and, therefore, don't truly appreciate the benefits the company is providing. To help increase employee retention, your job is to clarify these benefits for the owner.
- Ask for the opportunity to be the company's benefits PR person. Then, be ready to prepare a benefits overview, attach a dollar value to the package, and present the package to the employees.

What they don't know

Tell your prospect that most of their employees are dangerously underinsured. People tend to rely on their benefits package to cover all their anticipated insurance needs. It is important that employees realize that the business owner cannot be responsible for handling all of their insurance needs. Explain to your prospect the deficiencies in the company's disability coverage. Point out that critical illness is one of the major causes of personal bankruptcy. Remind the owner that long term care and life insurance are always less expensive when purchased at a younger age.

Ask for the opportunity to offer these supplemental products using payroll deduction. The owner might ask, "Why should I do that?" Your answer: "Because they need it, it's the right thing to do, they will appreciate you, and they won't leave your employ. That will result in increased profitability for your business."

After you have done your job, explained the benefits, and enrolled employees in the supplemental benefit plan, you head back to your office and call your group insurance buddy. Arrange to bring the group specialist to meet the owner. The business owner may now be more willing to let you quote the coverage. Why? You have developed a relationship. Your expert does the group work and you take a piece of the commission. That's the practical way to sell group insurance!

Chapter 72

Customer Or Client?

I was very impressed, early in my career, when my first general manager referred to people who bought our policies as "clients" rather than "customers." As a young man I believed that clients were people who did business with "professionals" such as lawyers or accountants. My first GM, however, set me straight: as financial services people, we too are professionals!

He advised me that we were not just looking for one sale from our prospects, as is often the case in businesses that deal with "customers." He also said that we were not in the transaction or retail business. That's why the insurance companies pay us the compensation. They recognize that their insurance products are not bought (by customers)—but are sold (by professionals to clients).

Also, the insurance companies are not in the "servicing" business. That's why we, the financial services professionals, do what we do. My first GM explained that my goal is to develop a lifetime relationship with my policyholder. One in which they come to me for financial advice—a relationship in which I become part of the individual's "financial team." I was excited. What an opportunity!

Many in the financial services business still take that approach. Their prospecting funnel is always full due to the referrals generated by their "clients." Others people working in our business take the "transaction" or "customer" approach. Make a sale—hit the road! It just doesn't make sense. It's also not fair to our clients (unless, of course, the individual requests such a "customer" relationship).

This is not problematic for the advisor who is ready to hang up his/her spikes. It _is_ problematic for the advisor who wishes to build his "practice" continually. You see, seniors have "Baby Boomers" who will soon be "junior seniors". Their kids are now looking for products that produce upside potential without downside risk. The days of the "Go Go Internet" stock market are over. Boomers lost money, as most of us did, and now they want to put a portion of their "savings" dollars into products that we offer.

But, how do we get in front of them? Go to our "clients?" Hold on! What if we only have "customers"? We will enjoy <u>no allegiance</u> from customers! They will shop the market and not give referrals, especially not to their kids!

It's not too late to turn your customers into clients. Now is the perfect time to reflect on how you operate your practice. Here's what you do: call all of the people who purchased a policy from you and set up a review. It's cost-effective, client friendly, and the right thing to do. Best of all, it will generate additional business—sometimes from them; sometimes from referrals. Don't become dependent on lead companies or seminar attendees. These are but a part of your practice. The advisor who is perceived to have "clients" will surely be more successful than those who just have "customers."

Chapter 73

Give 'Em A Ham Sandwich!

A man walks into a restaurant and sits down at a table. The waiter comes by and immediately starts going through all the specials of the day. The customer tries to politely interrupt but to no avail. The waiter keeps talking. Finally, the waiter is finished and says he will be back after the customer has a chance to think it over. The customer tries to stop the waiter but can't get his attention.

Finally, the waiter comes back and says, "Have you made up your mind?

Customer: "Yes. I'll have a ham sandwich."

Waiter: "I wish you would have told me sooner. We don't have a ham sandwich."

Customer: "Oh well, I'll just leave."

Waiter: "Don't leave! Let me tell you what's just like a ham sandwich."

Too late. The restaurant lost the business! What's the point?

ASK QUESTIONS! Find out what the customer wants. Also, make sure the customer/client knows what he/she is asking for. Did the client definitely want a ham sandwich, or would he settle for something that tastes like a ham sandwich? Maybe the customer just wanted something simple, plain, easy to remember—not really a ham sandwich, just something familiar. Perhaps it was price that motivated the customer— he knows what ham sandwiches cost, and maybe that's all he has to spend.

We need to do a solid job of interviewing our clients!

Today, we have access to vast amounts of information, much of it "information overload." Most of it is not relevant to our sales presentations. Think about it: are you, for example, an investment expert? Do you use all of the historical and hypothetical information in your annuity or SPL sale? Are you hammering away at investment principle?

Why are you doing this? These people are not talking to you about their investments. They are talking to you about their savings dollars.

<u>SAVINGS DOLLARS = SAFE DOLLARS.</u>
   <u>SAFE DOLLARS = SIMPLE PRODUCTS.</u>
      <u>SIMPLE PRODUCTS REQUIRE SIMPLE PRESENTATIONS.</u>

<u>SIMPLE PRESENTATIONS BRING ABOUT EASY DECISIONS.</u>

Easy decisions mean:

If he or she wants a ham sandwich…give 'em a ham sandwich!! Don't try to sell them a T-Bone! Something to *chew on*! Good, simple selling!

Chapter 74

Give The Kid A Chance?

The timing is perfect. There is a record number of recent college graduates looking for a business opportunity. That's right, I said "opportunity" not "pie in the sky." The current economic situation is leaving a lot of great new graduates in the dust. These people are bright, energetic, scared, disillusioned, but ready for a challenge. And by the way, they have "young ideas." So what can you do? How about multiplying yourself? Our industry has done a terrible job breeding new agents. It's just not being done to anymore. So why not take advantage of this deficiency?

Try this one on for size. We all invest in our businesses. We spend money on seminars, gifts, rent, computers, phones staff, advertising, travel, and much more. Nonetheless, I think bright young graduates could be your best investment. There are many activities that they are uniquely equipped for, trained for, and experienced in that they can help you with. For example,

- Designing and maintaining your website.
- Email marketing for new prospects and additional sales to clients.
- Learning the seminar business.
- Pre-qualifying prospects.
- Assisting you in the sales process.
- Selling along the way while doing administrative/management duties.

Consider a base salary, a bonus based upon new income brought into your firm, and an opportunity to "do what you do." Give this some consideration. Do a mini-business plan. For example,

- How much would you have to pay (invest)?
- Are you disciplined enough to train and manage?
- Are you open to new innovative youthful ideas?
- Do you want to grow?
- Are you ready for some excitement?

This will be the best decade for annuities and insurance. Why not have someone assist you in filling the funnel with new prospects? You may just have some extra time to do what you should be doing—enjoying your life! So, consider giving these "kids" (meaning absolutely no disrespect) a chance!

Chapter 75

"Listen Up!"

Many Americans are deficient in proper listening skills. This deficiency occurs at all levels. Most of us don't listen well enough at home with our families. Many of us don't listen to our friends and associates. Many students don't properly listen to teachers or professors. In our business, we can really be hurt financially if we don't listen to our clients and prospects.

What is good listening? Let's begin with what is <u>NOT</u> good listening.

Most of the time we are more interested in hearing ourselves speak rather than listening to our clients' ideas and wishes. I'm not saying we don't <u>want</u> to do what's right or help out. I'm saying that we may have a pre-conceived notion as to what our client needs and wants. Our client is being polite and listening intently. He/she doesn't want to interupt, so he/she remains quiet. The problem is we are not addressing the correct needs and we don't know what he/she desires.

STICK TO THE BASICS!

That's right! Don't try to explain every single product in your catalog, every advantage you can think of on the spur of the moment, every accomplishment you've achieved over the past ten years of your professional life. Just stick to the basics and listen for the cues that will help you win your client's business.

In our business, we sometimes miss these buying signals because we spend too much time flapping our yaps! So, "LISTEN UP!" Your client will feel important, your job will be easier, and you'll even make a little more money.

Good listening begins with asking leading questions and then shutting up long enough to hear the answers. Think of it this way: if in the typical client meeting you ask ten leading questions, your client will be talking at least 60% to 70% of the time. You will be listening all of that time. You will then be able to give short answers to his/her questions followed up with additional leading questions. By the end of the meeting you will know precisely what your client needs and wants and he/she will have received excellent counsel from you without all of the wasted time.

That's the magic of good listening—it's a win-win proposition! You have a client who wants to meet with you and you have solid information to help you guide and counsel your client to whatever goals you both have identified. And that's better than a steak dinner any day!

Chapter 76

Batteries Not Included

Did you ever watch a family member or friend open a great gift from you that didn't work because of the fine-print you overlooked—"Batteries Not Included"? I sure have! All too often we assume (or we forget to check) that the manufacturer has included the batteries. We are excited about picking out the gift. Sometimes we have spent hours and hours searching for it, and we want instant gratification. Well, the gift is still nice, but your loved one or friend can't enjoy it until he or she acquires that very necessary, final part—the batteries!

One of *Webster's* definitions of battery is "a group of two or more cells connected together to furnish electrical current." As human beings, we all need these "batteries" in our lives. We can provide our loved ones with all of the fine trappings of life—a beautiful home, new cars, a college education for our kids, and hundreds of other material items, but true happiness (that *electrical current*) doesn't happen unless you (the *battery*) is included.

It's the same in business.

You decide to embark on a new marketing venture. You attend those "power" seminars, you study the artfully designed materials, you spend lots of money developing and promoting your program, and then you quickly become dissatisfied because the results don't meet your expectations.

So, you begin to review the steps to find out what happened. You ask yourself many questions.

- Is the concept sound?
- Did the seminars explain the program in enough detail?
- Am I expert enough in the concept?
- Did I fall short in promoting the idea?

You may still feel good about your answers, but you still don't feel good about the results. You don't know what went wrong. So, you do one of two things:

1. BAG IT, or
2. DO IT AGAIN!

I would ask you this: "Did you remember to include the batteries?" <u>You</u> are the battery. Without your spark providing the needed electrical current, your success level will probably be sub-par. So, the next time you are looking at a new concept, ask yourself the following questions:

"Are you prepared to include the batteries?"

I hope that this simple analogy will "charge you up!"

Chapter 77

Performance Reviews

Performance reviews? When is the last time that you had one of these dreaded discussions? Usually, neither party is comfortable, and both go into the meeting in a defensive posture. If you are being reviewed, you know how uncomfortable it is. Maybe you have never been involved in a performance review, and, if you haven't, I would like to recommend a person who could conduct the best performance review for you. I'll give you the name at the end of this article.

I must admit, I did not have a single performance review during my first twenty years in business after leaving college. Well, that's not exactly true. My wife gave me the review, and thank God that she did! I really think that performance reviews can be very helpful when conducted with a <u>positive</u> attitude. Remember, the employee is always on his/her best behavior because the performance review determines his or her next year's raise in pay and/or bonus amounts. In other words, you may experience a lot of a—kissing going on!

In our business, however, we don't usually encounter this situation because we make an honest living—we <u>earn</u> commissions! What a concept! The more we work, the better we do. The better we do, the more we make. Heck! You can make more than the President of the life insurance company (a lot of you do that now), and no one can drop your pay or "freeze" your compensation—you control all of that! There is another unique thing about our profession—"the more good you do <u>for your client</u>—the more money you earn." Now isn't that an interesting concept?

I tip my hat to the insurance, annuity, and financial services representatives—one of the last bastions of the free enterprise system. Oh, the name of someone who would be the best person to conduct annual performance review? You guessed it—that person is <u>YOU</u>! You are the boss—you are the person who controls everything you do. Who knows you better than you, and who will be more honest with you? I highly recommend it!

Chapter 78

"Everybody's Talking About Me…"

Remember that song? It went like this—"Everybody's talkin' 'bout me; can't hear a word they're saying; only the echoes of my mind." I trust that a good percentage of you are old enough to remember that song. It's good basis for this essay. Why? Because everybody *is* talking about you—whether you know it or not.

Can you hear or do you know what they're saying about you? If not, it's time to find out, because their thoughts are how you are positioned in your marketplace. What if their thoughts are not how you want to be perceived? What if their thoughts are wrong or diametrically opposite of what you do or are different from your mission statement or platform? I think we'd better start investigating changing perceptions and branding or re-branding.

The end of the business year is a great time to reflect on past performance and great time for introspection. But virtually any time of year is a good time for such analysis. Here's a little drill to find out whom we really are and, more importantly, how we want to be known. Here goes:

1) Write a statement about how you <u>think</u> you are positioned in your marketplace.
2) Write a statement indicating how you would like to be known or perceived.
3) Who are you?
4) What is your business or what do you do?
5) Who or what is your market?
6) What needs do your clients have? What clients' needs do you satisfy?
7) Who or what is your competition?
8) How are you different from your competition?
9) Why you? Why should your prospects and clients do business with you as opposed to the competition?

Everyone has a reputation. It could be good; it could be bad, or it could be indifferent. We need to be concise in our answers when asked, "What do you do?" We have to be focused. Our answers must also lead to profitability. Compare yourself with successful people in your business. Compare yourself with the ones who are not successful. Define your niche, develop a mission statement, plan your work, and work your plan! Everybody's talkin' 'bout you...make sure it's "good" talk...profitable talk!

"Until Next Time ... Good Selling!"
Raymond J. Ohlson, CLU

What they're saying about Ray Ohlson:

"Let me introduce you to my friend and business-acquisition genius, Ray Ohlson. You'll find his insights and wisdom in the pages of this great book. Use this book, and it's like taking home one of America's great sales leaders!" — Dan Seidman of SalesAutopsy.com, "the sales horror-story guy!"

"When people are introduced, many nice things are said about them. Ray Ohlson is the real thing! But, not everyone knows Ray as a great family man and fun-loving friend. He is one of those special people who has succeeded at everything he has attempted from sales, management, to agency building, and as President of a major insurance company. All of these aspects of Ray contribute to make him the complete package. He has the positive attitude, integrity, and creativity that everyone wants in a leader. He is innovative, touch- and tough-minded, but he also unselfishly accepts the suggestions and ideas of those around him and likewise shares the credit with them. I've known and worked with Ray for over 30 years. I've not only learned a great deal from him, but he has been an inspiration for me in my career. But, most of all, I'm proud to call him my friend," — George Beatrice, CLU, RHU, Business Benefits, Inc.

"Ray Ohlson, an extremely successful Ball State Graduate, continues to serve on the Advisory Board of the Center for Actuarial Science, Insurance & Risk Management. His passion regarding the insurance industry and our university is remarkable." – Steve Avila, Ph.D., Co-Director, Center for Actuarial Science, Insurance and Risk Management, Miller College of Business, Ball State University